A Practical Guide to Parenting in the Digital Age

How to Nurture Safe, Balanced, and Connected Children and Teens

Winifred Lloyds Lender Ph.D.

ISBN 13: 9781495945724
ISBN: 1495945723
Library of Congress Control Number: 2014903194
CreateSpace Independent Publishing Platform
North Charleston, South Carolina

For my parents, Marlene and Richard,
Whose encouragement and love always ground me.

For Daniel and my three boys,
Whose energy, laughter and love sustain me.

Contents

Foreword

In my fifteen years of work as a psychologist with children, adolescents, and their families, I have seen the emergence of significant concern among parents as the digital age has come to fruition. Parents are concerned about the effects of digital media on their child, how to regulate digital access, and how to train their child to be a responsible and safe consumer in the cyber world. Many parents who have an arsenal of good parenting skills feel at a loss about how to navigate issues related to the cyber world. In part, the parents of today did not grow up with role models of how to parent around digital issues, as the digital world did not exist then as it does now. Moreover, the complexity of the digital world causes some parents to shrink from it and thus from parenting around it. The result is that some parents feel paralyzed to create any boundaries around digital usage in their home while other parents are so fearful of it that they ban it entirely from the home.

In my practice, I found that supporting parents in accessing the basic parenting skills they have honed in other areas, and applying them to digital use, has been extremely effective. Parents have come to see that they do have an effective skill set that can be applied to the seemingly overwhelming web of cyber issues today. Parents can learn to harness their skills to parent without fear around digital-age issues. In this book I present in simple and clear language the steps parents can take to use the basic parenting skills they have already developed to create a successful plan to manage digital access in their home. The plan can be adapted to fit any parenting style and can change over time. My goal is to empower parents to feel unafraid and to face head-on the inherent benefits and risks of the cyber world as it relates to their child.

One

Introducing the Problem

The May Family:

Dee and John are the parents of two boys, aged twelve and sixteen, and a daughter aged eight. They came for support for their boys, who they called "distant" and "disengaged from the family." Upon discussion it became clear that the parents felt the boys were being pulled into the digital world all the time, and this caused them to feel the need to police the boys' activities. The end result was a parent-child relationship that was negative and defined by anxiety and defiance.

"It really is overwhelming," said Dee. "I feel like I am a prison warden always managing the boys' time on their phones and social media sites. I have this nagging sense of anxiety that they may be doing something wrong, and I feel like a prison warden always checking on what they're doing, yet trying to act like I am not checking. I'm worried that my young daughter will soon be acting the same way. It makes me feel anxious and sad. John says he feels like the boys would always rather be on their computers or phones than engaging with him. 'I am competing for attention with the boys' phones and the Internet. It is like they are always waiting for a text even when we are together as a family. No matter what we are doing, I always feel that they will happily stop our activity for a text. It is frustrating.'"

This family is a typical one and their story highlights the pressure that the digital age can impose. They all felt disconnected, angry, and anxious and yet unsure of how to move forward.

The Parker Family:
Mary and Steve are the parents of a thirteen-year-old girl, Ashley. Their competing beliefs about how to parent Ashley around digital access is causing stress in the family. Mary says that Ashley is a smart girl "but she gets caught up in Instagram and Facebook and can't seem to think straight. She doesn't realize that what she puts out on the Internet will always be there and predators could see some of the photos she sends out. We need to protect her now and make sure she doesn't make any mistakes by not allowing her to text at all." Steve agrees that the digital world can be dangerous, but he feels the way to make sure Ashley learns to behave responsibly is to give her some freedom and then monitor how she does. Both parents agree that their different ideas on how to parent Ashley in the new digital age are causing the entire family great stress.

The Parkers are not unusual in that digital access has become an area of conflict for parents and children but also between parents. When parents don't agree on a course of action they experience a great deal of stress and conflict around digital access decisions.

Overview and Introduction to the Basic Principles
The emergence of the digital era, just like other significant new technologies before it, presents new challenges to parenting. When a new technology is introduced, parents need to discover a means to parent around it and often may feel alarmed. However, applying simple parenting strategies can support parents in facing the onslaught of this new technology, learning to appreciate its vast benefits and the parenting issues it presents. In simple language, ten guiding principles are presented here to help parents navigate through the maze of decisions that confront them

in the digital era. While the emerging technology is complicated, parenting around this new technology need not be.

Hands-on resources and worksheets are included to illustrate the principles and provide parents with the knowledge to parent without fear in this high-tech era. Parents will learn to construct from the ground up a digital floor plan and how to craft a digital use contract to support their child in being a mature consumer of digital media. Also included are troubleshooting points to deal with speed bumps and roadblocks along the road. A continuum of resources from highly restrictive to less restrictive are discussed to allow parents to find a set of standards for parenting in this new age that is consistent with their current parenting style. The goal is to provide a roadmap to help parents navigate this new parenting front in a way that acknowledges the digital world's positive qualities as well as its potential dangers.

Applying basic parenting skills, many of which parents already have honed, will make parenting in the new digital frontier much clearer and simpler. Most parents already have the knowledge and skills in their parent "toolbox" to successfully parent in this new age but are just unaware of how to apply these tools to the issues presented by the digital era. Parents can become overwhelmed by the new technology and forget to apply the basic parenting strategies they have used to confront other childrearing issues. This book serves as a reminder to parents of the basic principles they may already be familiar with and how to harness their strength to parent effectively and without fear in this new era of technology. The ten guiding principles to parent without fear in the digital age are:

1. Create a positive digital floor plan
2. Know the technology—the pros and cons
3. Develop digital access restrictions
4. Develop digital access expectations
5. Establish a digital access contract
6. Be consistent within yourself and as a team

7. Give reinforcement and consequences
8. Maintain balance
9. Practice what you preach
10. Know when enough is enough and when to seek help

Each of these ten principles is described in depth. Parents will see elements in each principle that they are familiar with and may be using in a different parenting context. For example, being consistent within yourself and as a team (Principle 6) is a concept parents experience daily related to other parenting issues such as toilet training, homework completion, bedtime routines, and curfew times. The concept of giving reinforcement and consequences to shape behavior (Principle 7) is also a common parenting tool that most parents already use to decrease off-task behavior when completing homework, increase independence in daily routines such as getting ready for school, and increase appropriate dinnertime behavior.

When taken one step at a time, the principles build a solid foundation for establishing a digital use plan in the home that is personalized to meet each family's needs and parenting style. Taking time to understand and take ownership of each principle, using the worksheets provided, and exploring the examples lays a solid foundation upon which each subsequent principle can be developed to create a strong digital parenting plan. Each plan will be personalized to meet the family's specific needs and parenting style, but will maintain the universal principles.

Two

Principle 1: Create a Positive Digital Floor Plan

Parenting in the digital era requires a thoughtful digital floor plan. The digital floor plan of your home, or the location of all the digital access points, can either greatly support your digital parenting plan or sabotage it. An important first step is to evaluate the digital floor plan of your home, assessing where the media access points are in the home. You need to carefully consider your digital floor plan as this can increase or decrease your chances of putting in place a digital plan that will be successful, making your child a safe and good cyber citizen.

In mapping the current digital floor plan of your home, look at computer access, Internet connections, television access, chargers for cell phones, and any other media outlets (such as CD players, iPods, etc.). Consider where the access points are and whether they make sense given your lifestyle as a family. In general, having all media access points in a central family location is recommended. A central charging station in a family-focused location, such as the kitchen or family room, is optimal. This allows for one consistent location for digital items to be stored, which increases your ability to monitor usage and cyber behavior.

Second, having a computer with Internet access only in a central family-oriented location is also recommended. By having access to the Internet in a central location you increase your ability to monitor the restrictions and expectations you will design; you are also able to observe firsthand any negative responses that may occur in your child as they explore the cyber world. In addition, having social activity in the vicinity of where the Internet is accessed will make it easier for your child to seek balance from the cyber world. If you have additional computers in the home, consider having them not connected to the Internet, serving primarily as word processors. If you have a Wi-Fi system with laptops, you can enforce the use and charging of the laptops in the family central locations of the house.

Television is also best in a central location where usage can be monitored and parents can interface with a child about what they are watching. Thirty-six percent of children aged zero to eight have a television in their bedroom (Common Sense Media 2013). Research bears out the fact that children with televisions in their rooms tend to watch more television (Kaiser 2008), and we can assume the majority of this television time is not closely monitored by a parent. Moreover, a television in a child's room is associated with decreased activity and an increase in obesity rates, propensity to use tobacco, and poorer school performance (Common Sense Media 2008).

Carefully evaluate where your television access points are in the house. A television in a child's room can lead to significant problems with sleep. Television can cause difficulties falling asleep and staying asleep and decrease the total sleep time of children (Mindell and Owens 2010). Television has also been found to increase the presence of nighttime anxiety and night-mares in children (Mindell and Owens 2010). Moreover, in this always connected, hyper-stimulating cyber world, it is important for a child to have relaxation time that does not involve digital media before bed so they can be alone and process the daily events without being hyper-stimulated. Falling asleep alone is an important skill that children need to master (Ferber 1985). Using a television to help a child drift off to sleep not only can interfere with sleep but also does not allow a child to self-soothe, a skill that can be important in managing everyday stresses and upsets (Ferber 1985).

Teaching a child to fall asleep on his own without a parent or digital device present requires time and effort, but it will pay dividends in the end. A child who gets used to falling asleep with a television or laptop playing a movie not only may have lesser quality and quantity of sleep, but also will become dependent on the television or laptop to sleep. They will associate the television or laptop with sleep and will require it to be on if they wake up in the middle of the night, so they can fall back asleep again. Learning to be "turned off" and not connected to the digital world is an important skill our children need to master, and not having a television in their bedroom supports this goal.

Always maintain charging of all digital items at night outside of the bedroom. Allowing a child to charge a cell phone or computer in their room, regardless of what restrictions you place on their usage, is problematic and can lead to significant sleep problems that in turn may impact on school performance, behavior, and mood. These devices are inherently stimulating, and the light emitted from them can provide physiological stimulation that is incompatible with the relaxation required to sleep.

In their *Clinical Guide to Pediatric Sleep Problems*, Drs. Mindell and Owens encourage parents to ban all electronic devices from the bedroom before sleep and during sleep hours. "Other screens (desk and laptop computers, handheld devices, electronic gaming systems, cell phones) not only provide cognitive and sometimes physiological and physical stimulation that interfere with the relaxed state required for sleep initiation but may provide enough light exposure to suppress the normal evening surge in melatonin and thus further delay sleep onset. Parents should be strongly encouraged to keep electronic devices out of (or remove them from) the child's sleeping environment" (23).

You will need to reevaluate your digital floor plan over time. As children age and show responsible use of digital media, you may decide to change the digital access points in your home. For instance, you may decide to allow more digital access points that aren't as centralized as you develop a comfort level to meet the restrictions and expectations you will develop. Keep in mind, however, that moving digital access to a private location can increase the chances for overuse or misuse of digital items and can lead to less family time. Always consider starting with a centralized digital access plan first.

Example 1 presents the digital floor plan for the Evans family. Mr. and Mrs. Evans came in for support about how to enforce rules and build trust with their sons, who seemed distant and disengaged from their parents. After an intake, it became clear the boys spent many hours alone in their rooms with their computer or cell phone and were not interacting much with their parents. Mr. and Mrs. Evans were unsure how to monitor their sons' digital usage to ensure they were safe, yet also give them some independence and not feel as though they were always checking on what the boys were doing in their rooms. When asked to complete the Digital Floor Plan Worksheet (Appendix A), the Evanses presented the information that follows.

Example 1: Evans Family Digital Floor Plan

The Evanses live in a two-story house. They have a television in each of their boys' rooms as well as their own bedroom. In addition, they have a computer with Internet access in the kitchen and in their eldest son's bedroom. They do not have a central charging station; all digital items are charged in the bedroom of their owner at night. Mrs. Evans said that the boys use their cell phones as alarm clocks and thus need to have them near their beds throughout the night.

When the Evanses completed the second part of the worksheet focused on troubleshooting, they began to see the inherent problems with their digital floor plan. They started to appreciate that their plan actually encouraged the boys to stay in their rooms and not interact with their parents, who were typically in the kitchen or family room after school and after dinner. Moreover, they saw that their digital floor plan was making it impossible to monitor their sons' digital access without "checking" on them all the time because their plan set their sons up to engage with digital devices in their own rooms. In addition, the parents realized that allowing their sons to have access to all their digital devices after bedtime was a recipe for failure. Not only would the boys be tempted to text their friends or surf the Web if they couldn't sleep, but the light the devices emitted could actually interfere with their sleep responses.

Once the Evanses realized how flawed their digital floor plan was, they were ready to make some changes. Using the worksheet, they designed a new digital floor plan.

Example 2: Evans Family Revised Digital Floor Plan

In the Evanses new digital floor plan, the televisions have been removed from the boys' rooms and one television has been placed in the family room. This allows the Evanses to congregate together to watch television and to monitor what their sons are watching. It also eliminates the problem of having their sons use the television to fall asleep instead of drifting off to sleep in a relaxing non-digital manner. In addition, the Evanses removed the Internet access from their sons' bedrooms and decided to have Internet access only in the computer in their kitchen. Mr. and Mrs. Evans reasoned that the computers in their sons' rooms could be used for word processing for homework assignments, while the computer in the central family location could be used for Internet research and digital free time, which could be monitored easily in the kitchen. The parents also devoted a section of counter space in the kitchen to a charging station where all digital devices would be charged at night.

The Evanses decided that as a family they would all begin to leave their digital devices in the charging station when they entered the home and ensure they were there prior to bedtime. Mrs. Evans purchased two alarm clocks for her boys that emit little light, allowing for an appropriate means to awaken in the morning. The revised plan is a more sensitive digital floor plan that supports the parents' ability to monitor and enforce a digital family use plan.

Mr. and Mrs. Evans initially received some negative feedback from their boys about changing the family digital floor plan. However, within a week and a half of instituting the new floor plan, Mrs. Evans remarked that the boys were "more engaged with the family," "helping in the kitchen," "talking about their school day," and "not rushing up to their rooms after dinner." Mr. Evans noted that he felt his sons were better rested in the morning and seemed "more relaxed." Changing their digital floor plan allowed the Evans family to alter more than just their digital use patterns. It supported the family in changing their interaction patterns. It moved the family toward one another and allowed them to connect in ways they had not in the past.

Establishing a positive digital floor plan is an important first step and may call for you to make some modifications in the digital access points in your home. Take the time now to set up an effective digital floor plan; it will pay dividends as you implement your digital use contract. A digital floor plan that allows for access to digital media in central family locations enhances your ability to monitor your child's digital usage and increases the probability that your child will be a good and safe consumer of digital media. Moreover, a floor plan that allows for a digital-free bedroom (charging of digital devices outside the bedroom at night and no television in the bedroom) will support a child's ability to self-soothe and sleep better. A digital floor plan that addresses the points mentioned in this chapter is a powerful vehicle that can not only alter digital use patterns, but also greatly impact on familial patterns of interaction and yield a greater sense of connectedness.

Summary:

1. Your home's digital floor plan, access points in the home for all digital media, can enhance or sabotage your digital parenting efforts.

2. Digital floor plans that allow for digital charging stations and digital access in centralized family locations, such as the kitchen or a family room, provide for the most supervision of your child's digital use and behavior.

3. Consider only allowing Internet access in a centralized location and having other computers, without Internet access, available for word processing usage in more private or quiet locations.

4. Television in a child's room does not allow for adult monitoring and can lead to problems with sleep.

5. Charging of all digital items should occur outside the bedroom at night. Access to digital items in the bedroom and the light they emit interferes with sleep and can impact negatively on daytime mood and behavior.

6. Evaluate your digital access floor plan over time. As children grow and you assess their ability to meet the digital restrictions and expectations you develop, you may make modifications that allow access in less centralized locations.

7. A digital floor plan can affect familial interaction patterns.

8. Changing a plan to allow for more centralized access of the Internet, central charging stations, and removing televisions and cell phones from bedrooms at night can yield a greater connectedness among family members as illustrated in the Evans family case study.

Three

Principle 2: Know the Technology – the Pros and Cons

Once you have organized your digital floor plan to support successful parenting, you can establish a basis of knowledge about the cyber world. This foundation will be essential when it comes time to develop a specific plan around digital usage (see Chapter 6). Taking some time to learn the fundamentals of this new technology will be an important first step that allows you to develop a sound digital family plan.

Parenting around any issue requires some basic knowledge of the subject. You need not be a great tennis player to support your child in developing a passion for the sport and becoming better at it. However, you do need to have some fundamental knowledge about it (i.e., what gear your child will need, how to find a pro to teach them, what age is a good age to start, how and when to communicate with the pro about next steps). And the more time your child is engaged in an activity, the more important it is that you understand the activity at some level. The striking finding (Kaiser 2011) that children aged seven to eighteen years are spending seven and a half hours per day in front of a screen (television, cell phone, Internet, iPod, Gameboy) under-scores the fact that knowing about the digital world is essential.

Often parents feel overwhelmed and anxious by the amount of new technology out there and thus decide not to learn anything about it. Amanda, a single mother of three, exemplifies this belief: "I have no idea about all this new technology. It is complicated and constantly changing. I feel like I won't let my kids go into a dangerous situation without being able to protect them in the real world, so why would I ever allow them to be free on the Internet, which can be very dangerous, if I can't protect them." Amanda's fear is common, yet it is important to remind yourself that digital life will probably be of great interest to your child and will likely be an area that continues to captivate them for the long term. The more knowledge you have about the digital world, the more you can harness its power for your child and ensure they are well protected.

In fact, the American Academy of Pediatrics in 2011 began encouraging parents to educate themselves about the different digital items their children use and to monitor their children's social media usage. The academy also encouraged pediatricians to educate themselves about these areas so they could best support the families they see. Knowing some basic information about the cyber world is essential to making rules around cyber usage and staying connected with your child.

By reading about the cyber world, you will come to learn its vast benefits. You will see it as a vehicle to obtain knowledge, to stay current in many areas, to connect with others, to feel support, and to explore areas of information that are of interest to you. In short, you may come to see it as a powerful tool that can enhance your life. Recent research supports that social media sites can offer opportunities for community engagement of teens, foster one's individuality, enhance individual and collective creativity, provide a venue for self-expression and connectedness, and enhance their communication skills (O'Keeffe and Clarke-Pearson 2011).

Teens can find others in the virtual world that share their feelings or have the same problems and seek support. At the same time, you will learn the negative effects of the digital world. You will come to see that when overused or misused it can lead to insomnia, anxiety, cyberbullying, depression, and introversion (Mindell and Owens 2010; Kaiser 2010). While the Internet and social media sites don't create these problems per se, the ease of access and speed of communication can magnify the intensity and frequency at which these issues evolve. Like any new technology, parents need to become educated about the full scope of positives and negatives. Knowledge is power.

There are several ways to educate yourself about the cyber world and its benefits and inherent threats. Common Sense Media (www.commonsensemedia.org), a no-profit organization aimed at promoting digital education and advocacy, is a wonderful resource. This group has a website full of information and tutorials about the cyber world. In addition, books about the digital world that provide an overview without being too complicated exist. Appendix B has a complete list of these recommended resources.

Once you achieve a basic level of understanding about the cyber world and learn some of the lingo, you are an informed consumer. You can appreciate the benefits of the cyber world, including the access to information, the means to connect and collaborate with others, the sense of community support, the ability for creative expression, the role of self-exploration, and the educational value. You can engage in discussions with your child about the cyber world and read about new issues as they emerge. By talking to your child about cyber issues you are showing them you have a basic knowledge base and an interest in an area that they have an interest in as well. Moreover, you are underscoring your awareness of the digital world that is important to them and thereby connecting with them. By opening up non-threatening communication on digital topics you allow for free communication that is non-punitive and increase the chances they will talk to you about the good and bad that happens in the digital world.

Staying current on digital issues is important. This allows you to be proactive; instead of waiting for a problem to emerge you can anticipate it and react in a timely manner. The more you can learn in advance of an issue, the more time you have to be thoughtful and to develop effective rules. To stay current, you can subscribe to technology updates or search for new media or technology updates on your favorite newspaper website. If you want to know what the current issues are relating to Facebook, you can Google the term "Facebook" and "news" and then read the stories that emerge. You can also use your favorite print copy newspaper and review the technology section, or buy a subscription to a technology magazine like *Wired, Computer Companion,* or *PC World.* Having a subscription to a digital magazine in the home allows you to be current and engage in conversations and debates with your children about the latest trends. Appendix C contains a complete list of magazines that focus on digital issues.

Amanda, the mother of three who hoped to "protect" her children from the perils of the Internet, found that learning about the digital world actually reduced her anxiety. "The more I learned, the more I knew, and the better I felt," she said. "I saw that there are risks in the cyber world, but I also realized that it has so many advantages. I want to be able to help my children be good digital citizens, and I feel like I can learn how to do this alongside them."

Always remember that knowledge is power. Although it may feel frightening to try to integrate new information, armed with some basic knowledge you will be in a good position to offensively develop a digital use contract. You will be able to parent from a position of knowledge and power as opposed to fear and uncertainty. Moreover, you will show your child that you are learning about an area that interests them and will have this arena to connect in.

Summary:

1. It is important to have some basic knowledge of the digital world, as this is an arena your child will spend a lot of time in. This knowledge will inform your digital family plan.

2. Use the online and print resources listed in this chapter and in Appendix B to gather some basic information about the digital world, focusing specifically on understanding new vocabulary.

3. Engage in discussion with your child about the digital world, and invite them to teach you about this new area.

4. Stay current on happenings in the digital world by checking news websites for updates on Chatroulette, Facebook, Instagram, Myspace, Twitter, Vine and other like terms or by subscribing to a digital focused magazine (see list in Appendix C).

5. Remember, knowledge is power!

Four

Principle 3: Develop Digital Access Restrictions

Many parents talk about how establishing digital access rules can become a dance of negotiation, pleading, and tears each day. Mary, a mother of two, speaks to the exhausting nature of constantly trying to invent and redefine rules around digital access in the home: "It just feels like every day is a new battle around if the kids should get their free computer time, how much, and when, depending on homework and afterschool activities. They are always asking me for time, and I get so worn down I just say yes because I'm too tired to organize a plan and they never stop asking. It doesn't seem like it should be so hard every day. I wish there didn't have to be the constant negotiating each and every day."

The need to constantly decide about digital access is time consuming and tiring and often feels "unfair" to both the child and the parent(s). A better practice is to develop a consistent set of rules in advance to avoid the cycle of requests, negotiations, and tears. When children and parents are clear on the rules in advance, children will begin to internalize the expectations and self-regulate.

With a solid digital floor plan in place and basic knowledge about the digital world, you can develop a set of clear restrictions around digital usage. As a parent you have developed a set of restrictions or limits for other parenting issues such as food, bedtime, and homework. You may parent around some issues with greater strictness and other issues with more lenience. Part of being a parent is determining how important it is that your child master a certain set of skills, and this informs how you parent around those target behavior goals. For example, if table manners are very important to you, your family dinner time may involve many reminders about behavior at the table, restrictions about behavior at the table, and consequences and reinforcers for table manners. As you become informed about the digital world you will incorporate this knowledge with your general parenting style and determine the extent to which you will use restrictions in your digital family plan.

The guidelines presented here will allow you to create digital restrictions along a continuum from highly restrictive to more lenient. It is important that whatever restrictions you chose to adapt feel congruent with your parenting style. It is also possible you may move from a rather restrictive set of rules to a more lenient set as your child grows older or as you feel more secure in their ability to manage their cyber-behavior.

In considering digital restrictions, you should address the following questions:

1. Amount of time of digital access (20 minutes, 60 minutes)
2. Type of digital access (Internet, television, iPod, cell phone)
3. Location of digital access (central family location, private room)
4. Timing of digital access (until a certain time at night or after homework is completed).
5. Contingencies (digital access is dependent on homework completion, doing chores)
6. Breakdown of digital access (homework versus enjoyment)

In developing a complete set of restrictions, you need to follow certain steps. Taking time to work through each step is important to establish effective restrictions. The four steps are: consider chronological/maturational age, evaluate the child's existing schedule, assess your ability to monitor restrictions, and incorporate the restriction components.

Step 1: Consider child's chronological and maturational age

First you need to think about the age of the child. Generally speaking, the younger the child, the less digital media they should be exposed to. The American Academy of Pediatrics recommends no screen time for children aged two and under. Screen time can increase gradually with age.

In addition to the chronological age of your child, also consider their maturational age. Is your thirteen-year-old son developmentally like other thirteen-year- olds, in terms of his cognitive and social-emotional skills? This is an important concept as it underscores the idea that it doesn't matter what everyone else is doing, it matters what is right for your child. If your child is younger developmentally than their chronological age, consider this as you develop their restrictions.

Step 2: Evaluate child's daily schedule

A central question all parents ponder is "How much time should my child be devoting to digital access given their school time, homework, afterschool commitments, and family time?" Before you can really answer this question, look carefully at your child's present schedule. Taking the time to evaluate their schedule and its balance will help inform you as you move toward establishing restrictions around digital access time.

The Daily Schedule Worksheet in Appendix D will help you determine the right amount of screen time for your child. This worksheet takes you through the process of establishing how much time each day your child is already committed to certain activities (school, homework, sports, transportation, sleep) and assesses how much time remains each day. Parents and the child can complete the worksheet together, or they can complete it separately and then compare their perceptions and negotiate one schedule that best reflects the reality.

This activity is not meant to be taxing, as in definitively allotting minutes to each activity; rather it is supposed to provide an overall sense of your child's daily commitments and the balance of physical activity, schoolwork, family time, and leisure time. This exercise may also inform changes, unrelated to digital access, that you decide to institute in your child's daily life if you find they are overscheduled, lack free time, or have days that contain no physical activity or family time.

As schedules vary by the day, it may be necessary to produce more than one schedule to reflect commitments on various days. Once you determine how much free time remains daily, you should factor in time for meals (hopefully family meals that allow for conversation) and family time. In addition, be sure to include non-digital wind-down time before bed. This self-soothing time can enhance sleep quantity and quality (Mindell and Owens 2010).

In organizing the schedule, ensure you allot sufficient time for sleep. Sleep is often under scheduled, and children and teens who don't sleep enough can show signs of anxiety, attention issues, depression, and obesity (Mindell and Owens 2010). Appendix E has a list of sleep requirements by age, although some children may need more or less. When assessing how much sleep your child is getting, ensure that the time reserved for sleep is actually being used for sleep and that digital devices do not take away from this time. A recent study (Polos et al. 2010) found that teens sent an average of ten texts per school night from ten minutes after lights-out to four hours after lights-out. Clearly, the presence of a digital device in the bedroom at night can negatively affect the amount of sleep your child is getting.

The time that remains each day after you deduct all the commitments—ensuring for adequate sleep time, relaxing time prior to sleep, family time, school commitments, homework, and any other commitments your child may have—is the existing free or unscheduled time. This time or part of it could potentially be devoted to digital free access time. Example 1 provides the Daily Schedule of Brenda. Her parents, with Brenda's help, completed the worksheet to assess her schedule and daily free time.

Example 1: Brenda's Daily Schedule
Using the Daily Schedule Worksheet to determine free time and potential digital free access time:
Brenda, age 14
Daily Schedule (Monday, Wednesday, and Friday)
Getting ready for school and breakfast: 60 minutes
School time: 6 hours
Transportation to and from school: 20 minutes
Homework: 1 hour 30 minutes
Volleyball practice: 2 hours (4 times a week)
Piano practice: 30 minutes (3 times a week)
Family dinner: 45 minutes
Family time: 1 hour (play games, read together)
Chores: 15 minutes
Pre-bed relaxing reading time (non-digital): 30 minutes
Sleep time: 9 hours

Total committed time on average school day: 22 hours and 50 minutes
Total sports time: 8 hours per week
Total homework time: 7.5 hours a week on average
Total family time: 9.5 hours per week
Total free time (potential screen time): 1 hour, 10 minutes per day

Once you have completed the sheet and obtained a total free time amount, determine how much, if any, of this time should be digital free access time for your child. Before you set aside time for free digital access, take a moment to reflect on the entirety of your child's schedule. Assess the overall balance of their day. Are they spending time in physical activity, with the family, engaged in a hobby/musical instrument? Are they getting sufficient sleep each night? The more variety they have each day, the better. Each day they may not achieve overall balance of activities, but the goal is to have their entire week present variety and a good balance of physical activity, intellectual pursuits, family time, and relaxing time.

Brenda's schedule, Example 1, is one that is well balanced. Clearly, Brenda, as with many of our youth today, is very busy and has little free time. However, her schedule reflects a good balance between physical activities, hobbies, family time, school, and homework. If you feel this variety is achieved and time remains, consider allowing some digital free access time if this is something your child enjoys and you can monitor it.

A word of caution: be careful not to schedule every minute of your child's day. It is not only acceptable but actually a goal to let a child have free time and figure out how to fill that time in creative (non-digital) ways. As Dr. Wendy Mogel in her book *The Blessing of a Skinned Knee* states, "Children need a chance to build up their boredom tolerance muscle. Allow him the pleasure of staring out the window, of throwing a ball around without a uniform or a team or a score, of counting raindrops without turning it into a multiplication quiz" (29-30). Oftentimes a child may be perplexed when told they have free time and may be at a loss as to how to fill it. This is a skill a child needs to develop, and allowing some of this time each day can encourage the growth of this skill. Make sure you allot some free time in their daily schedule so your child can develop this important skill.

If you review the Daily Schedule Worksheet and find balance has not been achieved, yet free time remains, look for opportunities to establish greater balance. For a child who is not doing physical activity, you might want to use part of the free time for a walk, throwing a football outside, or completing physical chores outdoors. For a child who has a lot of sports on their agenda but lacks a hobby, consider introducing time for listening to music or learning to play chess. You can introduce these options to gain better balance in the day and also maintain some unstructured free time that they must fill. The example of Laura that follows is illustrative of a schedule that is not well balanced.

Example 2: Laura's Daily Schedule
Using the Daily Schedule Worksheet to determine free time and potential digital free access time:
Laura, age 12
Daily Schedule
Getting ready for school and breakfast: 60 minutes
School time: 6 hours
Transportation to and from school: 30 minutes
Homework: 2 hours
Dinner: 30 minutes
Chores: 15 minutes
Pre-bed relaxing reading time (non-digital): 30 minutes
Sleep time: 9 hours

Total committed time on average school day: 19 hours, 45 minutes
Total sports time: 0 (except PE in school 2 times a week)
Total homework time: 8 hours
Total family time: 0
Total free unstructured time: 0
Total free time (potential screen time): 3 hours, 15 minutes

As can be seen in Laura's schedule, she has some free time, yet her committed time does not show variety. She is spending the majority of her committed time in school and doing homework and no time engaging in any afterschool sports, hobbies, or musical instrument practice. In addition, there is no mention of family time in the schedule. Assuming that all her remaining time should be used for digital access creates a very unbalanced schedule. It is worthwhile to look for ways to increase Laura's physical activity daily. Scheduling a half hour for outdoor play, dancing at home, or yoga would be a good starting point. Introducing some hobby, such as a musical instrument, singing, chess, or drawing each day, would also achieve better balance. It will be very important, too, to look at the daily routine and find ways to schedule quality family time.

It is optimal to have the family eat dinner together and have some fun family time after dinner. In addition, allowing Laura some free time to do whatever she wishes (as long as it is not digital or dangerous) can help her be creative and learn to deal with boredom. By adding these additional elements into Laura's day, the balance is better and she still has some screen time. Below is a revised schedule for Laura.

Example 3: Revised Balanced Schedule for Laura

Using the Daily Schedule Worksheet to determine free time and potential digital free access time:

Laura, age 12

Daily Schedule

Getting ready for school and breakfast: 60 minutes

School time: 6 hours

Transportation to and from school: 30 minutes

Homework: 2 hours

Afterschool exercise: 1 hour (3 days of ballet, 2 days walk with Mom)

Dinner with family: 30 minutes

Family game time: 45 minutes

Guitar practice: 15 minutes

Chores: 15 minutes

Pre-bed relaxing reading time (non-digital): 30 minutes

Sleep time: 9 hours

Total committed time on average school day: 21 hours, 45 minutes

Total sports time (ballet 3 times a week and walk with Mom 2 days): 1 hour each day

Total homework time: 8 hours
Total family time: 1 hour, 30 minutes
Total free unstructured time: 1 hour
Total free time (potential screen time): 1 hour, 15 minutes

Laura's revised balanced schedule contains physical activity each day. Some of this is a structured ballet class and other days it is a walk with her mother. In addition, her new schedule contains a family dinner and family game time each night. Time has been added each day for guitar practice that Laura will do with her father, combining some family time and a hobby together. The schedule has one hour of unstructured free time, otherwise known as time to get bored and be creative. Even with these additions, time still remains (one hour, fifteen minutes), some of which could be used for digital access free time.

When you complete the Daily Schedule Worksheet you may learn that your child actually has little, if any, free time. The worksheet may reveal how overscheduled your child is. Adam's schedule below (Example 4) is illustrative of many overscheduled children. He has many activities, very little family time, too little time to wind down for sleep, and very little sleep time.

Example 4: Adam's Daily Schedule
Using the Daily Schedule Worksheet to determine free time and potential digital free access time:
Adam, age 13
Daily Schedule
Getting ready for school and breakfast: 60 minutes
School time: 7 hours
Transportation to and from school: 30 minutes
Homework: 4 hours
Drum practice: 30 minutes a day
Morning drum band: 1 hour a week
Afterschool sports: 2 hours
Transportation to and from sports: 30 minutes

Language tutoring: 1 hour, twice a week
Family dinner: 30 minutes
Family game time: 45 minutes
Chores: 15 minutes
Sleep time: 5 hours

Total committed time on average school day: 24 hours
Total sports time: 2 hours each day
Total homework time: 4 hours a day
Total family time: 1 hour, 15 minutes
Total free unstructured time: 0
Total free time (potential screen time): 0

Adam's schedule is one of a child that is overscheduled with schoolwork, homework, tutoring, music, family time, no free time, no relaxing time prior to bed, and too little sleep time. Moreover, the fact that Adam is spending four hours on homework almost every night is concerning. Parents need to evaluate if this is actually on task-focused work. If he is really working for this period of time, the parents would meet with the school to ascertain why it is taking Adam so long to complete his homework each night and what the nightly time allotment is expected to be for homework. It may be that Adam really is not focused during the entire four hours but is only productive for two of the hours, which is consistent with what the school anticipates. He might need better supervision when he does his homework, a less distracting location to complete his homework (a digital-free quiet room), and/or motivation to finish his homework more quickly (free time).

Very importantly, Adam is getting only five hours of sleep each night. At age thirteen, Adam requires about eight and a half to nine and a quarter hours of sleep nightly (National Sleep Foundation). He is developing a large sleep deficit each night. It may be that it takes him so long to complete his homework because he is over-tired, which makes it hard for him to focus and learn. Through closer monitoring and support, Adam's parents may be able to decrease the amount of time he spends on homework each day, potentially eliminate an afterschool activity, and yield more time for sleep, relaxing time prior to sleep, and free time. Once they have established some free time they can assess how much of this time, if any, will be allocated to digital free time.

In assessing how much free time your child should devote to digital access, consider the finding (Kaiser, 2010) that on average children and teens aged eight to eighteen are spending seven and a half hours of screen time daily (Internet, cell phone, iPod, Gameboy, other video games, etc.). If you think about the amount of time a child spends in school, doing homework, transportation, sleep, and eating, it seems probable that many of these children and teens are spending the vast majority of their unscheduled time in front of a screen. The drawbacks of excessive screen time include anxiety, depression, attention issues, and obesity (Mindell and Owens 2010). The most significant drawback of excessive screen time is that it limits the amount of interactive family time, investing in the here and now as a family. This time is linked to improved mood and academic performance.

Having completed the Daily Schedule Worksheet you will have a sense of how balanced your child's daily schedule is and what free time they have. Knowing your child's age, maturational level, and your parenting style, you can determine how much of their free time you feel comfortable with them spending on digital devices. Remember that none of these restrictions is set in stone. Restrictions should be fluid and change over time as your child ages, as their cyber-behavior develops, and as you develop a sense of security in their ability to be good cyber citizens.

Step 3: Assess your ability to monitor restrictions
If you determine that your child's daily schedule is balanced and there is free time you want to allocate toward digital access, think about how you will monitor the access. If you allow access you may need to clarify the amount of access time, timing of the access,

location of the access, and any contingencies for the access. A restriction will only be effective if it is enforced. You will need to assess your ability to enforce restrictions. If you develop a restriction you can't enforce, the restriction will not be useful and may lead to upset and confusion. The following is an example of an unenforceable restriction and an enforceable restriction.

Example 1: Unenforceable restriction:
Jamie will be allowed 1 hour of Internet time in his room before bedtime.

Example 2: Enforceable restriction:
Jamie will be allowed 1 hour of Internet time in the kitchen from 5:30-6:30 p.m. each school day.

The first restriction is unenforceable for a number of reasons. First, the fact that Jamie will be allowed to have digital access in his room makes it difficult for a parent to monitor the content he explores as well as the amount of time he is online. The second restriction is more enforceable. It allows for access in a central location at a time when parents should be present in the kitchen to help monitor the content and time Jamie is online. This second restriction will likely be more successful and allows for supportive interaction between Jamie and his parents.

In designing digital restrictions, also consider your child's past behavior. Let the adage "the best predictor of future behavior is past behavior" guide you. If your child has had issues limiting their digital access or following restrictions in the past, you may assume that this will continue to be a challenge. In keeping with this knowledge, you will need to design restrictions that support your ability to supervise your child and ensure rules are followed.

Now that you have taken into consideration your child's chronological and maturational age, their schedule, their past behavior, and your ability to enforce restrictions, you are ready to craft restrictions around digital access. As a result of considering these factors, you may have decided not to allow digital free access, either because your child is too young (chronologically and/or maturationally), does not have time in their schedule, or you are unable to monitor this digital access effectively. It may be that after weighing these considerations you have decided your child is old enough, mature enough, has time in their schedule, and you are able to enforce a digital access plan. In this case, you will need to address the following issues when you craft restrictions.

Step 4: Incorporate the restriction components
1. Amount of time of digital access
Based on the Daily Schedule Worksheet, how much free time does your child have and how much of it will be devoted to digital access time?
2. Type of digital access
What type or types of digital access (Internet, video games, iPod, cell phone) will you allow during this time period?
3. Location of digital access (central family location, private room)
4. Timing of digital access
When will the free digital access time occur? Looking at your child's daily schedule, when is the optimal free time for him or her? Remember, this time should not occur right before bed. Also consider your ability to monitor access at various times of the day.
5. Contingencies
Is the digital access contingent on another activity? Must homework be fully completed before free digital access time begins? Do chores need to be done before this digital time starts?
6. Breakdown of digital access for school versus enjoyment
You may find that your child needs digital access to complete their homework. You will not want to limit this digital time if it is necessary to complete homework and thus should parcel out digital free time from digital homework time.

Two examples of restrictions follow. Example 1 depicts a restriction that does not address the restriction components previously described. Example 2 speaks to the restriction components.

Restriction example 1: John will be allowed 1 hour of Internet access time to complete all homework and play each day in the family room.

Restriction example 2: John will be allowed 30 minutes of free time on the Internet in the family room after his homework is completed and before dinner. If he has no homework, he will be allowed half an hour of free Internet time in the family room before dinner.

A quick reading of the two restrictions should bring to light that the first example is problematic. The restriction does not clearly delineate the type of digital access, timing of access, if the access is contingent on some other activity, or separate homework digital access from free-time digital access. In this example, a child is allowed only one hour of total Internet and digital time for both homework and free play. It may be that one hour is just not enough to complete homework, and thus the child is not allowed any free access digital time. In essence, the child may be penalized for doing a complete and thorough job on his homework with no free time on the Internet.

Alternatively, a child may rush through their homework in an effort to have "leftover" free-access Internet time prior to the one-hour limit. In general, if you are having the child complete digital homework in a location you can monitor and ensure actual homework is being done, there is usually no need to limit this time. There may, however, be instances when a child needs a time limit for digital homework, such as a child with attention issues who needs a structured time limit to better focus or a perfectionist who continues on indefinitely with their work.

The second example separates the free-access Internet time from the homework Internet time, avoiding the problem of having a child rush through their homework or being penalized for doing a thorough job on their digital homework and yet not having time for digital free access. In addition, this restriction clearly indicates that digital free access is dependent on homework completion and that the free access will occur at a certain time and in a family-friendly room that allows for supervision. The time of digital access is not too close to bedtime. The second restriction is not only clearer, but it will lead to greater success. A child will be better able to comply with this restriction and a parent better able to monitor it. Appendix F provides a worksheet for developing digital restrictions that address all the points discussed.

Designing restrictions for digital access use requires a careful assessment of your child's daily schedule. You need to assess whether they are overscheduled, if they are getting sufficient sleep, family time, and free time prior to thinking about allowing free-time digital access. Once you determine there is time for digital free access and you feel your child should have this access, consider their age, maturity, past behavior, and your ability to monitor their access. Designing restrictions that address the type of digital access, amount of digital access, timing of digital access, location of digital access, contingencies for digital access, and the breakdown of homework versus free-time digital access will be important. Taking the time to consider each of these factors will support you in establishing rules that are appropriate and tailored to your specific child and to your parenting style.

Summary:
1. Digital restrictions set rules around digital usage. They address the following: type of digital use, amount of digital use, timing of digital use, location of digital use, contingencies for digital use, and homework versus free-time digital use. You will adapt a set of restrictions that feel

appropriate to your overall parenting style. Some parents may choose to have very few restrictions, while other parents may choose a greater number of restrictions.

2. There are four steps in designing effective digital restrictions:

   a. Step 1: Consider your child's chronological age and maturity. In general, the younger the child the less digital time.

   b. Step 2: Assess your child's daily schedule using the Daily Schedule Worksheet (Appendix D). Determine if they are overscheduled, if their day is balanced, if they are getting enough sleep (Appendix E), have digital-free relaxing time prior to bed, and have family time and free time to get bored in their day. If free time exists you can allot it to digital access. If the schedule is not balanced follow recommendations in Appendix D.

   c. Step 3: Consider your ability to monitor and enforce digital use. Ensure that if you are allowing digital access, you will have a means to monitor it.

   d. Step 4: Incorporate restriction components. Ensure that restrictions address: type of digital access, amount of time for digital access, timing of digital access, location of digital access, if digital access is contingent on other activities, and separation of digital access of homework versus free time.

Five

Principle 4: Develop Digital Expectations

Now that you have developed a set of restrictions that are consistent with your parenting style and refer to the type, amount, contingencies for, location and timing of digital activities for your child, you can consider what expectations you have for his or her cyber behavior. Jack, a father of two, notes that he was so focused on what he didn't want his daughters to do in the digital world that he failed to define how he wanted them to behave: "There were so many things I told the girls not to do, and then I realized I never told them what they should be doing. They had a whole list of how not to behave but nothing really about how to act when online."

It is typically not enough to stipulate the amount of time your child can be online and what sites they can visit; you also need to define the specific type of behavior you expect when they interact online. Clearly defining the target behavior you expect for your child will help them meet the goal and can lead to a better cyber experience for them.

Expectations for cyber behavior are crucially important for children and teens, especially for those who visit social media platforms such as Chatroulette, Facebook Google+, or Twitter, which allow for open-ended and unstructured communication.

Appendix G contains a list of the most popular social media sites and applications for teens with a description of each (Common Sense Media 2013). There has also been a surge in popularity of photo and video sharing sites such as Instagram, Tumblr, Pheed and Vine. While each platform can determine its own age requirement for use, most indicate that users must be at least 13 years of age. This age requirement comes from the passage of the Children's Online Privacy and Protection Act (COPPA) of 1998 that stipulated how and when website operators need to seek consent from a parent or guardian and what responsibilities operators have to protect children's privacy. While a website can obtain consent for a child younger than 13, the amount of effort required to get parental consent is arduous and leads many operators to limit participation to individuals over 13. However, even though a site may list 13 as the minimum age required for site usage, users are only asked to self report their birthday or indicate that they are 13 years or older, making it very easy for children to lie about their age.

A quick review of the popularity of these social media sites and the problems encountered by users is useful. Social media sites are very popular, with 80 percent of twelve to seventeen-year-olds visiting them (Lenhart et al. 2011). While most of this group, 78 percent, reports positive personal outcomes from social media site interaction, 41 percent of this same group indicates at least one negative outcome. The types of negative outcomes most frequently reported are: mean behavior (88 percent), bullying (15 percent), and face-to-face argument with someone as a result of a social media contact (25 percent). In response to these negative outcomes, the majority of teens (91 percent) ignore the behavior and some (21 percent) join in (Lenhart et al. 2011).

Digital Onslaught: The Reality of Cyberbullying

The research suggests that online harassment and cyberbullying are common experiences for many teens. *Online harassment* is defined as aggressive behavior, harm doing, insults, denigration, impersonation, exclusion, outing, activities associated with hacking-stealing information, breaking into accounts, damaging websites and profiles, etc. (Willard 2006). Cyberbullying is online harassment that is repeated over time and typically involves a power imbalance between the perpetrator and victim, such as the perpetrator having better online skills, being older, or knowing more people online.

In its extreme form cyberbullying has led to the suicides of teens in several notable cases. In one such instance, a fifteen-year-old girl named Phoebe Prince who had recently emigrated from Ireland to Massachusetts hanged herself due to ongoing harassment on social network sites. In another circumstance, a fourteen-year-old boy, Jamie Rodemeyer, from New York committed suicide in 2011 due to repeated bullying online, and an almost fourteen-year-old girl named Megan Meier committed suicide in Missouri in 2006 after constant bullying on social network sites.

While these cases are rare, they can be useful as examples when you talk to your child, depending on their age and level of maturity, about the importance of good cyber behavior and what can happen when an individual or a group harasses someone online. Let your child know that telling an adult is a crucial step and one they will never be penalized for—even if they are unsure that what they see is actual harassment or cyberbullying, and regardless of whether the victim seems upset by the harassment. The outcome of the cases previously listed could have been different if a teen that knew about the bullying had told an adult.

Cyberbullying is on the increase both in terms of its frequency, the number of children and teens affected by it, and its scope (Cyberbullying Research Center 2013). This increase has led many schools to introduce regulations around cyberbullying and education about appropriate cyber behavior. Many schools have cyber contracts they ask students to sign which describe the type of online behavior expected of students using computers at school and at home.

Today the majority of states in the United States have laws against harassment, and some have laws against online harassment and cyberbullying. Some states have legal penalties for cyberbullying and online harassment that can involve suspension and expulsion from school as well as potential monetary fines. Some states allow a school to expel a child for cyberbullying on social media accessed in the home. It is worthwhile to know what your state's rules are and to let your child know as well. The cyberbullying Research Center (www.cyberbullying.us) is a good resource and has an up-to-date list of cyberbullying laws and policies by state. This information can provide an important reminder to your children that what they do online, even in the safety of their own home, can have significant and long-term consequences for them at school and in their community.

The anonymity of the cyber world coupled with the social psychology concepts of *groupthink* (Janis 1972, 1982) and *risky shift* makes the cyber world a prime breeding ground for cyberbullying. In the cyber world, teens are more willing to make decisions involving greater risk than the individuals who make up that group would alone (risky shift), which leads to more bullying, unkindness, and taunting than would occur in one-on-one situations in the real world. In addition, in the cyber world maintaining group cohesiveness and solidarity appears to be more important than considering the facts (groupthink), which can explain why teens often ignore it when other teens are cruel online or make threats to others.

Sexting: Sex in a Text

Sexting is the sending of sexually provocative (nude or near nude) texts, photos, or videos through the phone or email. Research shows that teenagers send sexually explicit photos to others due to peer pressure, self-esteem issues, as a romantic gesture, or to be rebellious. Overall, slightly more girls than boys send sexts, and at least one in ten teenagers has sent a sext; three out of ten have received one. Typically, teens and tweens send these texts or emails intending them to go to only one person. While they may consider these messages "private," the reality is that nothing sent via a phone or computer is actually private. If it can be copied or photographed, it can be sent to anyone. It is especially important that children and teens understand that photos sent via Vine or other applications where the photo is supposed to "disappear" after a given period of time, do not guarantee privacy. A photo of the image can be taken and it is questionable whether anything in the digital world really disappears.

Teens and tweens need to know that their reputation today is made up of their online or virtual presence and their real presence. Sexting can have significant implications for their online reputation for years to come. Once an explicit text is sent, the teen loses control of their virtual reputation. They will never know when and if that photo and message will be revealed to others. While sexting may make the teen momentarily feel powerful, by sending the text they are really losing their power and control.

Sexting can also be illegal. If your child receives a sexually explicit picture of a child under eighteen it could be considered child pornography, and you may be legally required to take it to the police. In addition, if your child receives an explicit text and they send it to others, they could be violating privacy laws. This can be a serious offense as distributing sexually explicit material related to a minor is illegal.

Explain to your child the legal ramifications of sexting as well as the potential implications it has on his or her reputation. Instead of preaching to your child about what not to do, talk to them about what they should do—how they should guard their privacy. To make the situation more real, you can search for teen sexting examples in your community on the Internet. Providing your child with a real-life example of someone in your community who had a horrible experience due to texting can make the issue real for them. In addition, discuss the specific steps your child can take if they are asked to engage in sexting or if they receive a sext. Have them role-play what they would say or do in these situations. Having the words that sound "cool" to get themselves out of a peer pressure situation can make a big difference. Let them know they immediately need to show parents an explicit message they received and delete it.

Online Predators

In addition to cyberbullying, which is generally perpetrated by children and teens, online predators (often adults) pose a threat to children and teens on the Internet today. Just as parents caution children about being careful for predators as they walk to school or visit the mall, so too must parents teach their children how to protect themselves from virtual predators. Enough is Enough (enough.org) is a not-for-profit group that aims to make the Internet safer for children and families. The organization cautions that "significant gaps exist between the Internet's dangers to children and the level of legal, enforcement-based and industry driven action dedicated to protecting our children" (enough.org). The organization's website contains detailed statistics relating to the incidence of sexual solicitations online.

For example, a study found that one in seven kids/teens receives a sexual solicitation online (Mitchell et at. 2007). Strikingly, this same study found that of those teens that receive requests to meet someone they met online, 16 percent have considered meeting their virtual "friend" in person while 8 percent report actually meeting someone they have only met online.

Clearly, children and teens need to be educated about the potential dangers of meeting people in the real world that they "met" in the virtual world. Children also need to be informed of the importance of guarding their personal information (full name, address, school name, location of activities they engage in). While parents may take it for granted that children know not to disclose personal information to someone in the virtual world, children may not make this connection. The virtual world, particularly social network sites, engender a feeling of community and closeness that children and teens can easily confuse with really knowing someone and their true background. In talking about the virtual world and when designing a digital family plan, parents must make this connection explicit.

These findings underscore the importance of establishing clear expectations for the type of cyber behavior you expect, what to do if a negative outcome is experienced, and how important it is to guard personal information online and never meet an online "friend" without first discussing this with a parent. The following cyber expectations are intended to address the problems teens may encounter online and especially on social network sites. They are comprehensive, and as a parent you may choose to include all of these or only some of them. These expectations should be considered as you develop your own set of expectations. A full list of these expectations is contained within Appendix H.

Expectations:
1. Use only respectful language (no profanity).
2. Treat others online with kindness and respect.
3. Let parents know immediately when someone has treated you unkindly online.
4. Let parents know immediately if a friend is being treated unkindly online.
5. Let parents know immediately if someone online, even if you don't know them, is treating someone unkindly or being treated unkindly.
6. Talk to your parents about anything that makes you feel uncomfortable that happens online or about anything you don't understand.
7. You will only share non-explicit/tasteful pictures with others online (define tasteful) and will let your parents know if anyone sends pictures that are explicit to you.
8. You will never send sexually explicit photos of others to friends and will immediately delete any if you receive them.

9. You will share only general information about yourself online but never disclose your home address, phone number, or school name to anyone online.

10. You will never agree to meet someone you "met" online without first checking with your parents. If your parents agree to the meeting, you will be sure that it is in a public place and bring your mother or father along.

11. You will not respond to any messages that are mean or make you feel uncomfortable. It is not your fault if you get a message like that. If you do, you will tell your parents right away so they can contact the service provider.

12. You will not give out your Internet password to anyone (even your best friends) other than your parents.

13. You will check with your parents before downloading or installing software or doing anything that could possibly hurt your computer or jeopardize your family's privacy.

14. You will be a good cyber citizen and will not do anything that hurts others or is against the law.

By developing expectations for your child regarding digital behavior, you allow your child to clearly see what the target behavioral goals are and may help them avoid a negative outcome and be safe in the virtual world. Having a clear model of what the expectations are helps children appreciate their target behavior and move toward this goal. Moreover, the expectations put a mechanism in place for communication whereby your child should let you know when there is a negative outcome online, whether it is directed at him or her or at others. This communication is essential. Taking the time to develop these expectations for cyber behavior will support your child in becoming a safe and kind cyber citizen.

Summary:

1. Digital expectations define what behavior is expected in the cyber world. It is not enough to tell a child what not

to do online; you must detail what you want them to do as well.

2. Research suggests that the majority of teens have some negative experiences online, and it is important to establish expectations that address appropriate behavior as well as instruct them to tell a parent immediately if someone is unkind online or if something doesn't feel right.

3. Predators exist in the cyber world, and children are solicited for sex or to meet predators online (enough.org). Establish clear rules around what information your child can release online, and inform them of the dangers of arranging to meet people they know only online. These are essential components of a digital family contract.

4. A sample list of expectations is detailed in Appendix H.

Six

Principle 5: Develop a Digital Use Contract for Restrictions and Expectations

Many parents have a very good idea of their desired digital access rules for the family, but they never actually formalize the rules on paper. Arianne, a mother of two, describes this: "We had all these ideas of what the rules were about using the Internet and texting, but we never actually put it all down on paper. It always felt like we were recreating the wheel when we needed to remind the kids about the rules, and then there was oftentimes some kind of argument about whether that was really the rule. I guess I felt as though I wanted to just be flexible and not commit to writing things down, but in the long run it seems like this led to more problems and misunderstandings. I thought a digital contract was silly, but now I realize it is really important."

A Digital Use Contract is the cornerstone of a family plan that addresses digital use. This contract contains restrictions and expectations for digital use as well as consequences for infractions and a system for evaluating success of the plan. This contract provides a clear enforceable plan for all those involved in monitoring a child's digital usage. The contract reduces your need to create rules and consequences on the spot and your need to respond to infractions when you may be emotional. The contract provides a fair playing field where children know what is expected and can work toward these goals and negotiate with parents around the restrictions if they choose. Armed with this contract, parents will have a concrete plan to guide them as they navigate digital issues and questions.

The contract may be extremely restrictive and extensive or brief and less restrictive, depending on each parent's parenting style and their family's needs. A family may start with a very extensive contract and then loosen the rules as their children get older and demonstrate responsible behavior online. Once you achieve an understanding of what a Digital Use Contract is, you can then fit it to your parenting style and family needs so it feels appropriate and workable. There is a continuum along which contracts can fall from extensive and restrictive to rather brief and less restrictive. Examples of contracts that fall along the continuum will be presented.

The process of developing a clear and enforceable contract takes time and thought and requires collaboration from the whole "team" (parents, siblings, child, caregivers). It is important to spend the time now thinking about and developing the plan, as a contract that is vague and not well developed can cause more confusion around digital use parenting issues. There are seven steps to developing a Digital Use Contract. Following each step and utilizing the worksheet resources will help you to craft a contract that is clear, enforceable, and successful in modifying behavior.

Step 1: Writing the rules
You have already developed some restrictions around digital usage that address the amount, type, location, contingencies for, and timing of digital access. Now you can phrase the restrictions

in a way that is clear, positive, and enforceable using the instructions that follow and the worksheet in Appendix H.

The way you state the restriction is very important. Always state the rule in a positive way that has minimal verbiage. For example, stating "Emily will be allowed one hour of total screen time (television, Internet, iPod) each day after homework is completed" is better than stating "Emily will not be allowed any more than a total of one hour of time on the computer, Internet, cell phone, or iPod each day but only after she has completed all of her homework." The first statement is phrased in a positive way, sending the message that Emily will be successful, and contains minimal verbiage; the second restriction sets the limit as punitive and uses too many words, which can confuse the message. Appendix I provides a worksheet for crafting rules around media usage and a checklist for evaluating the tone of language used as well as sample rules. Using this worksheet you can craft rules that will be positive and clear.

Ensure that the rules you create can be enforced and monitored by parents or other adults in the home with ease. In keeping with this, state a clear time limit and how it will be monitored (a kitchen timer or alarm clock set by the parents). If at all possible, the digital use should occur in an area that the parents can easily monitor, such as a kitchen or living room. The likelihood of compliance is far greater when a child knows they are being monitored, and the burden is far less for the parent when the child is visible. Setting up a child for success with the Digital Use Contract often requires that the digital use occur in a public area of the home, with parents or an adult nearby and a timer set by a parent in earshot.

Your last item on the contract should address the length of time the contract will be in effect. For example, you might want to note that the contract "will be in effect until summer break begins, at which time it will be reevaluated" or it will be "reevaluated in two months' time or sooner if needed." The goal here is to make sure the contract is responsive to new needs or schedules that may change. A child may be more willing to accept a plan that feels restrictive if they know it is not "forever" and parents are willing to reevaluate it at a certain point in time. Also, even the best-laid plans can fail, and if you find the contract is not working, you will need to retool it immediately. There will be more on troubleshooting and retooling rules when step 7 is discussed.

An example of rules around digital usage follows. As you read them you can see that they are clear, written in language children can understand, presented using positive language, enforceable, and set in place for a certain time period.

Example 1: Rules for Digital Usage:

1. Emily will be allowed one hour of digital time on her laptop, iPod, or the television each day after homework is completed in the kitchen.
2. Emily will use a kitchen timer to time her free digital access time.
3. The plan will be in effect until school is over in June or until any team members (Emily, her parents) decide that the plan should be retooled.

Example 2: Rules for Digital Usage:

1. John will be allowed 30 minutes of television time each school night in the family room after homework is completed.
2. John will enjoy any show he likes between 6:00 and 8:00 on channels 2-36.
3. This plan will remain in effect until March, at which time we will all reevaluate it.

While you can monitor, reinforce, and provide consequences for your child's digital access and behavior online at home, this will not be the case when they are out of the home. In the school setting, computers are generally filtered to block inappropriate sites, and most schools have policies about what is allowed in terms of cyber behavior. It is worthwhile to learn what filters are used and the policies and restrictions at your child's school as well as the consequences for transgressions. This information can be shared with your child. You can let them know that while you hope they will follow the rules for being a good cyber citizen when they are in the school, the school also has important rules about their cyber behavior. These rules may describe how they are to behave online regardless of where the computer they are using is.

Children and especially teens will also want to go online with friends. They may do this at your house, in which case you can specify that your restrictions and expectations hold true for everyone who uses computers in your home. Briefly let your child's friend know what the rules are, and ensure that your child agrees to abide by them, even when their friend is present. You can also monitor the activity if the computer is in a centralized family location.

Your child may also want to go online at a friend's house. You will need to decide how to handle this. You may or may not know what type of monitors their friend's computer has, whether it is in a centralized location, and if an adult monitors their usage. You can discuss this with your child. Let them know you expect them to hold to the restrictions and expectations you negotiated for the home when they are online in their friend's house. You will be less able to monitor this, of course, but having some guidelines in place can be effective.

You can also discuss with the parents of their friend what your home digital rules are and inquire about their rules. Children and teens may engage in more risky behavior in a group, so asking parents about their policies is appropriate. While this may embarrass your child or teen it is a very legitimate question, and if you find that there is no supervision or rules, or the parent gets angry at your question, these may be signs that this is not an environment you want your child online in. While it may seem initially scary to let your child go into the cyber world where you cannot monitor it, this can be a developmentally appropriate step for them. You want your child to gain independence in self-monitoring and be able to recognize and report when things do not go right. By allowing them to explore the cyber world from other access points you are giving them important practice that can support them in becoming good cyber citizens.

The following restrictions could address the issues of a child using a digital item at school or at a friend's house.

1. You will respect our restrictions and expectations around digital usage when you are at a friend's house or at our house with a friend online.
2. You will respect all the school rules around digital restrictions and expectations.

Step 2: Including the means of monitoring

The restrictions and expectations in a Digital Use Contract are only effective if you have a means of monitoring them. Parents often make the mistake of assuming that a contract is functioning—without checking. Some parents fail to identify monitoring techniques in the contract because it seems punitive to do so, or they keep monitoring techniques a secret from the child. In fact, not identifying how you will monitor compliance with rules and expectations is problematic on several levels. First, it may send a message to the child that it doesn't really matter if they comply with the rules and expectations. Second, if you don't spell out how you will monitor compliance, your child may feel their privacy has been invaded or they have been "tricked" when you do monitor their compliance. Third, failing to discuss monitoring of digital use in the contract goes against the whole goal of the contract. For all these reasons, it is essential to address how you will monitor your child's compliance with the Digital Use Contract's restrictions and expectations.

Monitoring techniques can be classified in two categories. One category is the low-tech means of monitoring digital use. This refers to discussions with your child about how to be a good cybercitizen, how to be safe online, checking the history of websites they have recently visited, "friending" your child on a social media site, and checking the social media profile of your child. These are considered low-tech as they do not require any special software or complex knowledge. Your child can show you how to friend them on a social media site and how to see the history of sites visited on the computer. It is recommended that at a minimum all Digital Use Contracts contain the following low-tech monitoring components.

Example of Low-tech Monitoring in a Digital Use Contract:
To ensure your safekeeping in the digital world, we will do the following:

1. We will periodically check what information is available about you online.
2. We will periodically check the history of the sites you have visited on the computer and on your mobile phone.
3. We will periodically check your social network site profile.
4. We will friend you on any social media sites you join.
5. We will periodically look at the texts you send.
6. We expect to be notified about any passwords needed to access your computer or mobile accounts.

Beyond these low-tech monitoring techniques, there are a host of more high-tech procedures that allow for greater scrutiny and more parental control. This type of monitoring includes setting parental controls on the computer or cell phone that restrict, filter, or monitor the type of sites that can be visited. For example, Self Control is a free software program for Mac users that allows parents to block access to certain websites for a period of time. This added level of monitoring may be useful for parents who feel they require more stringent monitoring techniques. Commercial products that support this type of monitoring are listed in Appendix K. An example of monitoring statements for a Digital Use Contract that contains this level of high-tech monitoring follows.

Example of High-tech Monitoring Techniques in a Digital Use Contract:

To ensure your safekeeping in the digital world, we will do the following:

1. Use parental controls on the computer and your mobile phone that block, filter, and/or monitor your usage.
2. Use filter systems that set PC game blocking by rating.
3. Use filter systems that limit access by time of day and daily time limits.
4. Use filter systems that provide keystroke and screen captures.
5. Use filter systems that provide detailed and graphical reports of online activity.

Step 3: Outlining consequences

You have already developed a set of restrictions and expectations for digital use as well as a means of monitoring these. You must now consider what the consequences will be for noncompliance. Clearly identifying these consequences in a Digital Use Contract is important. While parents may feel that having consequences in the contract implies that the child will transgress, stating consequences provides clarity for everyone. It is much better for parents and the child to be clear on consequences prior to an instance of noncompliance—a time when the parents may feel angry and the child may feel guilty and upset. Placing consequences in the contract eliminates the stress of having to figure out an appropriate consequence when you are upset due to your child's noncompliance. Moreover, the burden of having to decide on a consequence when other team members are not present is negated.

Parents who feel uncomfortable identifying the consequences in the contract should remind themselves that this actually helps a child be successful in meeting the behavioral goals and keeps the contract consistent. A parent can reinforce this belief to their child by saying, "We are sure you will be successful in meeting these goals. We have the consequences listed below because we know it is fair for you to know what they are." This message underscores the parents' belief that the child will be successful while showing the child that much thought has been put into the goals and consequences.

In considering effective consequences, keep in mind the primary things your child enjoys and values. Limiting access to these items can be a meaningful consequence that motivates better behavior. An effective consequence needs to be as immediate as possible so the child clearly connects the transgression with the consequence. It is important that the consequence be administered every time a transgression occurs. In addition, to be effective the consequence should be administered in a manner free from emotion and anger. Appendix I has a worksheet for developing restrictions and assessing if they meet the important criteria of being meaningful, immediate, consistent, and non-emotional. An example of consequences that meet these criteria follows.

Example of Consequences in a Digital Use Contract:
We know you will work hard to follow all the restrictions and meet the expectations in this contract. Below are the consequences we have designed because we know it is fair for you to know what they are.

1. If you engage in digital free time (accessing Facebook or sports websites) before your homework is complete, you will lose your digital free time the next day.

2. If you say unkind things online or use profanity online you will not be allowed to go on a social media site for a month.

3. If you use your digital items after bedtime, you will lose your digital free time privileges for 5 days.

4. If you don't stop using digital items when the timer sounds, signaling the end of your access time, we will subtract this time from your next day of digital free time.

You can craft a set of consequences that fits your parenting style. Consequences may be brief or extensive depending on what parents feel fits their child's needs and the way they parent.

Step 4: Testing the rules

Now that you have developed your restrictions, expectations, and consequences using Appendix H, a test run of the Digital Use Contract is recommended. You can ask another adult to read the contract assessing clarity of the rules, expectations, and consequences as well as looking for any loopholes or misunderstanding that may occur. Often times, an older sibling can be helpful in this process.

Once you are reasonably certain you have an appropriate, clear, and enforceable Digital Use Contract, you can set up a meeting to review the contract with your child. Give your child a copy of the rules and, depending on their age (both chronological and maturational), ask them to read over the rules independently and write down any questions they have—or else read the rules to him or her. You can also include siblings in this exercise, as they often are very proficient at devising exceptions to the rules and encouraging their siblings to test rules. Encourage the child to ask questions, and present some possible scenarios to ensure they understand the rules.

Returning to the example of Emily, who "will be allowed a total of one hour screen time after homework is completed in the family room," you could pose a set of questions such as: "Will

Emily be allowed screen time if she has no homework to do?" "Will Emily be allowed screen time if she has homework to do but forgot it at school?" "Will Emily be allowed more screen time if she has completed all her homework and it is only 4:00?"

The goal here is to explore all possible misunderstandings to ensure your rules are clear and enforceable. If you are preparing rules for more than one child, have each child pose their own questions and present them with anecdotes to make sure they understand the rules. It is important that all parents or other caretakers involved in monitoring the child's digital use access be involved in this process so that all adults have the same understanding of the rules as the child does. Appendix J contains a draft Digital Use Contract with questions from a child written on the contract.

Step 5: Revising and formalizing a contract

After your meeting, it may be necessary to clarify the rules if the children do not understand how they are stated or loopholes have been found. Once you have revised the rules, have the children review the new rules again. The time you spend during this phase will pay dividends later as you may avoid misunderstandings and potential problems in enforcing the rules. Once you are reasonably sure the child understands the rules, put the rules in contract form. Taking the time to make the contract look official reinforces to the child that it is an important document. Once the contract is produced, all team members should come together to do a final reading of the contract and sign it. Appendix L has copies of a finalized Digital Use Contract.

Step 6: Making the contract visible: providing a constant reminder

Once the contract is signed, post it in a visible area near the computer your child will be using. The visibility of the signed contract near the computer or charging station provides an added reminder for the child and parent of the agreement. Simply posting a contract in an area where the behavior you want to occur will occur can increase adherence with a contract. You can consider posting several contracts: one near the computer, one near the charging station, and one near the television.

Step 7: Troubleshooting

If you, your child, or other members of the team find the contract is not working, it is essential you reevaluate it immediately. Having a contract that doesn't work in operation only creates confusion and can lead to improper behaviors and expectations around digital use. In fact, having a faulty contract in place can be worse than having no guidelines at all.

If the contract is not working, let the child know that you are aware the contract is not working and that you will be troubleshooting to make it work better. Invite the child to tell you why the contract is not working, and ask other members of the team to give you their opinions as well. Give them a timeframe for when you will meet to discuss a new contract. The more quickly you respond to the problems, troubleshoot, and create a new contract that fixes the problems, the more you highlight the importance of the contract and your sensitivity to the team's concerns. In assessing why the contract is not working, review the checklist in Appendix I.

Summary of Developing a Digital Use Contract:

1. Sate the rules and expectations with little verbiage and in a positive way. Be sure that the rules and expectations can be monitored and enforced.
2. Consequences for transgression of rules should be clearly spelled out in the contract. For consequences to be effective they need to be immediate, consistent, meaningful, and non-emotional.
3. Address expectations for cyber behavior at friends' homes and at school.

4. Write down the rules on the worksheet and ask an adult to problem solve around loopholes with you. Have all members of the team review and agree to the rules. See Appendix I.
5. Present the rules to the children in advance and encourage them to ask questions. Clarify any rules based on the child's questions. See Appendices J and L.
6. Assess the child's understanding of the rules by presenting scenarios, and clarify the rules if necessary.
7. Once a child understands the rules create an official contract. Have all team members come together with the child to sign the contract. See Appendix L.
8. Post the contract in a visible place such as near the computer so there is a constant reminder for all about the rules.
9. Remember that to make the rules effective, you as a parent need to enforce and monitor the rules.
10. Make sure you reevaluate rules if the contract is not working (see Appendix I for troubleshooting ideas) or when it becomes apparent a change is required, such as during summer break, vacations, when children get older, or when their digital homework needs change.

Seven

Principle 6:

Be Consistent

One frustrated mom wrote: "My thinking was that we should be flexible about how much computer time the kids get. My husband and I could make a decision, depending on who was home, about how much time the kids would get. I thought this would teach them to be mature users and that they don't need to be bound by all kinds of rules. I guess I have learned that this doesn't really work well. I am always the bad guy because I usually give them less time than my husband."

As a parent you already know that rules, consequences, and reinforcers are only effective if all members of the team follow them consistently. Children learn early on with whom they can push the limits and who will hold fast to the rules. You may already be able to identify which member or members of your team are likely to enforce the rules—or not. Be vigilant in making sure the whole team understands the importance of following the Digital Use Contract consistently and accurately. If the contract is inconsistently monitored or enforced by a member of the team, it sends a message to the child that the contract is not important or worthy of being enforced. This message may in turn cause a child to be noncompliant with the terms of the contract.

Inconsistent reinforcement of a Digital Use Contract undermines the entire contract. It can make a child feel confused as to why some team members enforce the rules and others don't. It can also make a child feel angry that one team member allows them to be online for long periods of time while another provides consequences for this same behavior. Moreover, inconsistent enforcement can actually strengthen the behavior you are trying to decrease and set up an intermittent reinforcement cycle— the child doesn't know when they will be allowed to engage in a behavior so they continue to try because there is always a chance they will be allowed to do so this time.

An example of this is found in the way the lottery works. Some people play the lottery often because while they don't win, there is always that slim chance they could win and this motivates them to continue to play. In our scenario, a child may try to stay online past his allotted time, ignoring the rules, because it's possible a parent will forget to monitor him or fail to put forth the consequences spelled out by the contract. Once a child learns that rules are strictly enforced, the intermittent reinforcement of a behavior is lost and the behavior will begin to change to comply with the behavior goals in the contract.

Consistency in monitoring and enforcement of the contract across all team members (Mom and Dad enforce the same way) and within team members (being consistent as a parent each and every day) is essential to the success of a Digital Use Contract. You can expect that once you put in place a new contract, there may be an extinction burst, or an increase in the behavior you are trying to decrease or eliminate, as a child tests out the new contract and adjusts to a new behavior pattern. If the contract limits the amount of computer time, you may find your child trying to sneak in more computer time than they had even prior to the contract. This can be a natural occurrence as we attempt to change behavioral patterns. Anticipating extinction bursts, or an increase in the behavior you are regulating, you can be prepared to monitor closely, respond non-emotionally, and follow through with a consequence.

Let your child know that you appreciate how hard it can be to change behavior and that it will get easier with time. You can draw parallels for your child, detailing how when you tried to change a behavior (be more active, eat fewer sweets) you experienced how hard it was initially but then found it easier with time and enjoyed being able to change your behavior. You should also let the other team members know about the extinction burst and what consequence you gave. Maintaining a consistent team approach is imperative in dealing with any potential extinction burst and ensuring the success of the Digital Use Contract.

Summary:
1. Being consistent is essential to the success of the Digital Use Contract. Intermittent or inconsistent reinforcement of a Digital Use Contract, such as not responding to infractions at times, can sabotage the effectiveness of the entire contract. A child may maintain a behavior you are trying to change if they believe they will be allowed to engage in this behavior at times.
2. Ensure your team, particularly members who have difficulty being consistent in other parenting fronts, is aware of how vital consistency is with the plan.
3. Prepare for the possibility of an extinction burst—an increase in the behavior you are trying to change—when the plan goes into effect. Anticipate this possibility, monitor behavior closely, and respond with immediate consequences if needed.
4. Always try to respond non-emotionally to infractions. If you respond emotionally, your message may be lost in the emotion. Simply indicate what your child has done wrong and what the consequence is. Use the contract as a guide.

Eight

Principle 7: Give Feedback and Communicate

Positive feedback: we all need it, and your children most of all. Setting up a digital family plan is a perfect time to step up your communication and feedback, especially words of a positive nature. One father told me, "Nancy and I feel like we didn't talk to the kids enough about how they were doing following our digital contract. I guess we only really talked about it when something went wrong and one of the kids didn't follow a rule. Our oldest says that we only focus on negative things he does and aren't aware of how much he is really doing a good job following the rules."

It isn't enough to implement a clear and enforceable contract; you need to make sure the team (parents, other caretakers, siblings) supports the success of the contract through ongoing communication and feedback. The team needs to catch the child "being good" or complying with the rules and expectations of the contract. Find instances to acknowledge your child's compliance with the rules. Let the child know it can be hard to change behavior and you appreciate that they are working hard to make these changes. Positive reinforcement will increase the behaviors you hope to see, such as good cyber citizenship and complying with time limits for digital use.

Acknowledge transgressions of rules or failure to meet expectations. A child needs to know what they are doing wrong when they are doing it. Let a child know as soon as possible that they are not following the rules. Specify exactly what the child did that was noncompliant, showing them the contract as a visible reference. In addition, identify what their consequence is for this infraction. Present this information as unemotionally as possible. If you show emotion, your message may be lost by the emotion. Remember that the immediacy with which you identify an infraction and provide a reasonable and non-emotional consequence, the more successful the contract will be over time.

Working as a team means that you communicate on an ongoing basis, celebrate the success of the Digital Use Contract, and also troubleshoot if something is not working. Just as you engaged the team to construct the original contract, you need to engage them to monitor, enforce, and troubleshoot any issues relating to the contract. Check in with all team members on a regular basis and ask them how they think the contract is working. Do they see it as being effective and worthwhile?

Be cognizant of the fact that implementing a Digital Use Contract requires, especially in the beginning, more work from the team than prior to the implementation of the contract. The team members need to monitor, enforce, and oftentimes deal with some anger or upset from a child who may not like having limits set. Beyond the additional time you are asking the team to devote, you are also asking them to adopt a new style of parenting or caretaking; changing behavior is hard for anyone. Acknowledge your team's hard work and thank them. Let them know how much you appreciate their help. Remind them that the contract may be more taxing initially, but in the long run it will create a better environment for all.

Summary:

1. The Digital Use Contract will only be effective if you communicate with your child and the team about successes and infractions.

2. Find opportunities to catch your child being good or complying with the rules, and compliment them describing exactly what they are doing that you like. Reinforcing good behavior will actually lead to more of it.

3. Acknowledge any infractions immediately and unemotionally with consequences.

4. Let the team know you appreciate their work in monitoring and enforcing the contract. It can be hard for anyone to change behavior, and you are asking your team to do things differently now.

5. Remind the team that the contract will get easier in time and that the end goal—having a child who is a safe and good cybercitizen—is very important.

Nine

Principle 8:
Balance Is Key

Jason, a father of four, talks about how his children can't seem to get enough of the digital world: "It's really hard for my boys to stop and disconnect from the computer or their phones. The other night when I couldn't sleep, I walked by my oldest son's room and saw the glow of light coming out from the door. When I went in I found him watching videos at three in the morning."

Annette, a mother of three, describes her daughter's unease when separated from her cell phone, even briefly. "My daughter threw a fit when I said I wouldn't go back to get her cell phone she had left at home. We were only going to be gone from the house for a couple of hours, but she was acting like she literally couldn't live without her phone for this short time. It was scary to see her so out of control."

Balance is an important concept in parenting. As parents, we continually try to strike a delicate balance, not to be too strict or too lax, not to give too much support or too little. Parents try to impart a sense of balance to their children daily. We support their efforts at academics and athletics and reinforce their efforts in the arts as well. This same sense of balance needs to be taught in the cyber world.

The digital world is inherently difficult to create balance around because it is available and "on" 24/7. Not only is it always on, it has an immense amount of information, so it becomes easy for a child, or even a parent, to spend hours and hours in the digital world. Moreover, the information is novel and always changing, which makes it reinforcing to consume the digital information often. The digital world is a large and exciting social world for children and teens. They use it to connect with friends and often feel pressure to be online so they don't miss anything.

The draw of the digital world has been borne out in research. A recent Kaiser study reported that children aged seven to eighteen spend on average seven and a half hours of screen time (computer, cell phone, iPod, Gameboy) a day (Kaiser 2012). This means that these children are spending almost half their waking hours in front of a screen. When coupled with the fact that, on average, these same children are spending six hours or more a day in school and seven to ten hours sleeping, we can see that there is very little if any non-screen family time. Clearly, this pattern of excessive screen time coupled with school demands is not one that shows balance between family life and school/ screen time.

In addition, many children are overscheduled with school, and with their screen time added in there is very little time for a child to become bored and learn how to entertain himself. By scheduling every waking moment of a child's day with screen time or school, we may be robbing them of a very important skill: how to deal with boredom and entertain themselves.

The overuse of digital media has many negative effects. By virtue of the amount of time children spend onscreen, they have less time for outdoor activities and physical exercise. A link between amount of screen time and obesity has been established (Kaiser 2010). Furthermore, there is no or very little time for family interaction. Family time in many homes now revolves around each family member being plugged into their digital media devices in the vicinity of one another. It is not uncommon to find Dad on his iPhone responding to work email messages, Mom on her laptop corresponding with others, a son in his room listening to his iPod, and a daughter plugged into a Gameboy on the couch.

Excessive screen time may also lead to problematic social interactions. Children who tend to be introverts may find the virtual world of social interaction much less threatening and may use this to the exclusion of developing real social interactions. Children who are extroverts may find it hard to limit their social interaction online or limit their number of virtual friends. For both extroverts and introverts, the cyber world, especially social media, can become problematic.

As a parent you want to support your child in creating a balanced approach to the digital world, and first you need to acknowledge how difficult it is to do this. The allure of the cyber world is strong. But appreciating how hard it is to establish balance will make you more effective in creating guidelines and more prepared when infractions do occur. The goal is to help your child develop a balance each day of physical activity, schoolwork, social time, digital time for homework, and digital time for play. Each day may not have a perfect balance, but the goal is to have a week that supports a balance of each of these activities overall.

Perhaps Monday will be a day with less physical activity and social time and more homework and digital time for homework, but Tuesday may be a day with a lot of physical activity, social time, free digital time, and less homework. Establishing a balance takes time and careful consideration. Teaching your child how to establish this balance is an important lesson that they can use throughout their life. Appendix M has a Balance Worksheet for scheduling and a column for monitoring the success of finding balance each day. If your child has had an unbalanced or stressful day, they can be encouraged to try one of the relaxing activity options from Appendix N. These activities can also be used to wind down and relax before bedtime.

Teach your child not to feel bad if they have a day that is out of balance. It may be they predicted the day would be out of balance, perhaps due to final exams or a sports tournament, and thus plan to compensate the next day. The essential idea is that they recognize when a day is out of balance and are proactive in creating a better balance the next day. This recognition will allow them to self-monitor their digital usage and how it "fits" with their other demands and interests. Using the schedule to monitor balance will help make this process more apparent, and eventually a child will be able to "feel" when a day is unbalanced, without the use of the worksheet, and take steps independently to get balance back.

Summary:
1. The cyber world is an always "on," novel, and exciting medium that has a strong draw on all of us. It can be particularly hard for children and teens to learn to "turn off" the digital world.
2. Teaching your child to establish balance in their life between the digital world and the real world is essential.
3. Acknowledging to your child that this is a hard balance to achieve, but one that is necessary, is an important first step.
4. Use the Balance Worksheet, Appendix M, to support your child in developing a balance each day of their daily demands, including digital ones. The worksheet can be used for planning and then evaluating how balanced each day was and planning to create more balance the next day.
5. Use Appendix N for ideas of relaxing activities your child can do when their schedule is very unbalanced, when they feel stressed, and as a means to relax before bedtime or wind down after a stressful day.

6. The goal is for your child to realize that not each day can be balanced; final exams and sports demands may interfere on certain days, but the goal is to have an awareness of when things are out of balance and a mode for reining their schedule back into balance.

7. Achieving a sense of balance is an important life skill your child can use.

Ten

Principle 9: Practice
What You Preach

Dawn, a mother of two young girls, talks about the pull of the digital world for her as a parent: "I know I shouldn't be spending too much time checking my phone when I am with the kids at the playground, but I just feel this tug to take a peek. Last week I went to quickly check my email while my youngest daughter was playing, and then when I looked up again I couldn't see her. My heart started racing and it was horrible. I found her in less than a minute, but it really made me think about just leaving my phone in the car."

Marni, a mother of one son, also speaks to how hard it can be to model good digital behavior. "The other day I told my son to put his phone away and pay attention to us at the table, and he said, 'Why can't Dad put his phone away too? Why is it only a rule for me as a kid?' This really hit home for me."

As parents we know that we should practice what we preach. If we tell our child not to yell, we also should not yell. If we ask our child to be polite, we too should be polite. The principle is based on the fact that children naturally model what we as parents do, and this drive starts very early in life. Infants will model a parent's smile or movement and toddlers want to hold the car keys, talk on the telephone, or "read" the newspaper as their parents do. Many parents have been shocked to hear a young child say a curse word—and then realized they learned it from Mom or Dad when we used profanity in a moment of weakness. Responding "don't do what I do or say" typically does not work and may actually increase interest in the behavior we are hoping our child will avoid. All parents come to see that to get our child to "do as we do," we must model the behavior we want them to engage in—if not all the time, then as close to all the time as possible.

The concept of "do what I do" or "practice what you preach" holds true for digital use as well. It is not uncommon to see a family out for dinner in a restaurant where both parents are looking at their emails or talking on a cell phone and the children are either also on their cell phones or on a Gameboy or other digital gaming device. The parents are modeling that cyber usage in this scenario is expected and acceptable and also sending a message that it is more important than connected family time at the dinner table. As parents, we are the primary agents who can model appropriate cyber use for our child. We can display the right balance of digital use and family interactions and demonstrate the appropriate balance between the digital world and the real world. Some cyber usage goals that parents can model follow below.

Digital Use Rules for Parents:
1. *Put all digital items in a charging station when you enter the home.*
We can abide by the Digital Use Contract and charge our digital items in a family-centered area as soon as we walk into the home. We can also turn off cell phone ringers. We can immediately invest in our family when we enter the home and put our cell phones in the charging station. This demonstrates to our child that we can "turn off" from the digital world and be present in family life. By physically removing the items from our pockets or bags we are less tempted to accidentally or habitually check a cell phone.

2. *Establish a predetermined limited amount of time for digital use each day.*
Just as we ask our child to limit their digital usage to a certain amount of time, location, and time of day, we too can demonstrate our ability to limit and focus our digital usage. Parents can devote a limited amount of time each day or evening to checking emails or doing work and try to do this in a central family location so we are consistent with what we are asking the children to do. Determining that you will spend half an hour in digital activity each evening and then looking at the clock before and after you get online is an important check for you and sends the message to your child that you are practicing what you preach. Using a timer to clock our digital usage is a good first step in this process.

3. *Ban all digital items from the meal table.*
The family meal is a very important part of your child's life. In her book *The Family Dinner*, Laurie David notes that the family dinner is an extremely powerful tool that parents can harness to enhance the life of their child. Children who eat dinner on a regular basis with their parents have been found to do better in school, be happier, and be less likely to smoke cigarettes (David and Uhrenholdt 2010). Fully investing in the family meal is essential to reaping its benefits. This means being present and not being connected to a digital media device or checking one periodically. By charging digital items at home during meals (and turning the ringer off) you can be in the "here and now" at the table and enjoy all the benefits this togetherness can offer.

If you are dining out with your child, consider leaving digital items at home or in the car. If you must take them with you, turn the ringer off and pledge not to look at them during the meal (from the time you enter the restaurant until the time you leave the restaurant). Being present with your family entails turning off the digital world for a period of time during meals.

4. *Remove digital items from the bedroom at night.*
As noted earlier, keeping digital items at night in the bedroom can interfere with the quality and quantity of sleep. It is harder to fall asleep and stay asleep when the light of these items is in our room. Research has shown that the light digital items emit can suppress our sleep response (Mindell and Owens 2010). In addition, digital items in the bedroom can serve as a constant reminder of stressors or things we need to do. If we do wake up in the middle of the night, a digital item in the room can be a strong pull that may draw us to searching the Web or looking at emails, waking us up even more and making sleep a less likely possibility.

Use an old-fashioned alarm clock (not connected to a cell phone or email or texting capacity) to rise in the morning instead of your digital device. Establishing a buffer of non-digital use time for at least half an hour prior to bed and throughout the night is important in allowing us to wind down prior to bed; it also sets us up to get a good night's sleep. We can model to our children that we do not need digital devices to fall asleep and that they can actually impede sleep.

5. *Connect with your child non-digitally.*
Earlier it was mentioned that learning about the cyber world offers you an opportunity to connect with your child in an arena they enjoy. It is, however, essential to connect with your child daily in non-digital ways as well. A family dinner where digital items are banned is a perfect way to ensure you get this non-digital time daily. In addition, making time after dinner or before bed for old-fashioned non-digital games is a wonderful way to connect with your family, demonstrate a balance between the digital and non-digital worlds, and have some relaxing time prior to bed. Games such as charades, cards, Scrabble, Pictionary, chess, and checkers are perfect examples of non-digital games that have wide appeal for the whole family. Appendix O has a list of non-digital games for different ages that can be used to

connect as a family. Family time prior to bed is a relaxing way to reconnect and also helps your child disengage from the digital world prior to bed.

Consider instituting a Digital Free Friday Family Fun Night. As a family you can plan a dinner menu and activities for after dinner that don't involve digital devices. At first it might seem difficult to design an evening that is digital free, but after a few attempts it will become routine. You may find that your child at first resists a digital-free family night, but with time they may come to really enjoy this slow-paced family-centered night. Be creative and allow a different family member to take a turn planning the dinner menu and the after-dinner activities. Any of the games listed in Appendix O could be used as an after-dinner activity. In addition, weather permitting, your family could go on a walk to get a dessert, go on a star walk, have hot cocoa under the stars, tell family stories, or simply read a book together as a family. There are many options that allow you to connect in a digital-free manner as a family.

6. *Be honest about your digital usage.*
Perhaps the best message you can send your child about digital usage is that it is an ongoing balance you must work at. Some days you will achieve balance and some days you may not. Instead of covering up your digital use mistakes, use them as teachable moments. Tell your child how you did not charge your cell phone in the kitchen last night, and when you woke up in the middle of the night you couldn't resist checking your email, which caused you to become very alert and made it difficult for you to fall asleep again. Letting your child know that achieving a digital balance in life is hard work, even for a parent, is important as it reinforces that this is a challenge. Tell your child that you are going to keep working toward achieving a better balance; this reminds them not to give up, to move on, and to learn from mistakes. Explain that tonight you will definitely leave the cell phone charging downstairs, even if you have to walk downstairs

to do this before bed. This action reinforces the notion of continually trying to achieve balance.

7. *Know yourself and when you need help to control your digital usage.*
As a parent you need to know your limits and when you need help. Take the self-report Internet Addiction Test (www.netaddiction.com/internet-addiction-test) developed by Dr. Kimberly Young to measure severity of Internet addiction. The results of this measure will allow you to compare your digital use to others'. Even if you don't think your digital use is excessive, if others in the family indicate that you are "online too much" or are "disconnected from the family" you need to seek help to create a better balance. The power of digital devices is revealed in the fact that 53 percent of adults feel upset when denied access to a digital device and 43 percent feel lonely when they are not able to go online (Common Sense Media 2011). Consult with the family first and try to develop ways to respond to their concerns. Invest in truly following these seven steps just described on a consistent basis. Ask others to monitor you. Consider developing your own Digital Use Contract that you post in a salient location and attempt to follow.

If you find it difficult to comply with the seven steps for parent digital usage just discussed, are unable to be compliant with a Digital Use Contract, or continue to receive feedback from family members that you are "connected to the digital world too much," consider seeking professional help. Consult with a professional about how to create more balance in your life between the real world and the digital world. You may want to bring a family member to the first session to describe their concerns about your usage, and be prepared to detail the amount of usage you engage in, what you have tried to curtail your usage, and why you hope to change this behavior. A skilled professional can work with you to develop a plan to obtain better balance in your digital use. You may learn that you have not really been very present in the here and now of your family life and can develop skills to become more present.

Appendix P contains information about the types of different professionals you might want to consult about digital use issues. In addition, several questions are detailed that you might consider asking the professionals to determine which one you want to work with and what the process will be like.

Remember that the digital world has a strong pull for adults as well as children. It can be hard to disconnect from the digital world (and work that may be associated with it) and invest fully in the here and now of family life. Family members telling you that you are "always on the computer" and "not connected" with the family is the first step. Investing in achieving better balance and enlisting the support of your family is the second step. Seeking professional help is the third step in this process. Asking for help is not a sign of weakness but a sign of awareness. This can be a "teachable moment" for your child, a time to appreciate firsthand how to get help when there is an imbalance. You will also be showing your child how important family life is to you.

Summary:
1. Children will model their parents' digital behavior; doing what you want your child to do around digital use is essential.
2. Put all digital items in a charging station when you enter the home.
3. Establish a predetermined amount of digital time each day that you will engage in and time yourself to see if you comply with the limit you have set. Minimize as much as possible your digital time when children are in the home.
4. Ban all digital items from the meal table. Make sure cell phones cannot be heard at the table.
5. Remove all digital items from the bedroom at night; the quality and quantity of your sleep may increase. Use an

independent alarm clock, not a mobile digital device to wake up in the morning.

6. Connect non-digitally with your child daily. Having non-digital family time prior to bed is a perfect way to have family time and encourage your child to disengage from digital devices in anticipation of bedtime. See Appendix O for ideas of non-digital family games.

7. Be honest about your digital usage with your child. Use your mistakes as teachable moments to underscore for your child that achieving digital balance is a challenge, but one that you continue to invest in.

8. Know yourself and when you need help to manage your digital use. Take the self-report Internet Addiction Test (www.netaddiction.com/internet-addiction-test).

9. Listen to family members. If they say you are "too connected" to the digital world, consider seeking help. Appendix P has resources for finding a professional to assist you in creating more balance between the digital world and your family life.

Eleven

Principle 10: Know When Enough Is Enough and When to Get Help

Beth recalls how she came to realize that the digital world had taken over her son's life. "John seemed to be in a bad mood all the time. He was kind of jittery and never seemed to really be present when we were doing family activities. I brought him in to be evaluated for depression and wondered if he was taking drugs, but it turns out he was addicted to gaming on the Internet." Eric presents a similar picture of his daughter Ellie. "She was so intent on checking the social media sites all the time, and if she saw a friend who was doing something and didn't invite her she would get depressed. It was a cycle of wanting to check all the sites and then always feeling down after. It wasn't healthy, and she actually would go without sleep and food in order to stay connected on these sites."

The power of the cyber world has already been discussed. As an always "on," ever-changing social sphere, it has a particular draw for children and adolescents. The majority of children and adolescents, with proper support and supervision, can learn to enjoy and make use of the digital world in a safe and balanced manner. However, some children and teens develop significant difficulties related to their digital use.

The incidence of insomnia, depression, obesity, and anxiety has been linked to overuse of digital media (Polos et al. 2010). Children and adolescents can become addicted to digital access and may demonstrate withdrawal symptoms such as anger, anxiety, and depression and may lie or bargain to get access to the digital realm. For example, when a recent University of Maryland study asked students not to use digital media for twenty-four hours, a large percentage of students experienced symptoms similar to those of drug and alcohol withdrawal (ICMPA 2010). The child or teen may act as though they cannot live without digital access, even for the briefest time period. In fact, 38 percent of surveyed college students said they couldn't last for ten minutes before switching on some digital device (ICMPA 2010). This is a sign that our youth are feeling more than a preference for digital devices.

There is a fine line between a preference for using a digital device and a need to use one or an addiction to it. Children and adolescents can quickly cross this line if not monitored. Being aware of how much your child is using digital devices, monitoring their mood, and tracking their ability to comply with the Digital Use Contract are important steps to determining if their preference for digital use has become problematic. The Internet Addiction Test (www.netaddiction.com/internet-addiction-test) is a good resource to use to assess if your child's preference for digital use has become an addiction.

When you feel your child is overusing the digital world in an unhealthy or excessive manner, you need to act. The Digital Use Contract may not be sufficient in all cases. If you have a well-developed Digital Use Contract and are providing consequences and reinforcement but still feel your child's digital use is out of control, seek assistance. Consulting with a professional is a good first step to develop a plan. Make sure you are prepared to detail your child or adolescent's history of digital use and the amount of time they are spending connected. Bring a copy of the Digital Usage Contract you have used and a Balance Worksheet detailing your child's daily activities to help the professional assess what rules, expectations, consequences, and reinforcers you have used in relation to digital use.

Reaching out for professional help as soon as you identify that a problem exists that is not responsive to your parenting tools is essential. The longer you wait to access help, the more ingrained behavioral patterns will become. In addition, your concern and any other emotions will become magnified if you wait to seek help. Appendix P contains a list of resources for finding a professional who can support you with this issue and questions to ask to determine which option will be the best fit for your family.

If you decide you need to seek help for your child's digital usage, do not present this as a punitive option. It is not that the child has "failed" but that the team (parents, child, and other adults in the home) needs to develop better skills to manage the situation. Through consultation with a professional, parents and the child will learn different ways to manage access to the digital world and techniques for establishing better balance between the digital world and the real world. By sending a positive and hopeful message to your child about seeking help from a professional, you are setting him or her up for a successful therapy experience.

As noted previously, the cyber world is an incredibly reinforcing, always novel, and continually available social world. It can become hard for children and parents to effectively control their access to this enticing venue. As a parent, you know your child best and will know when the balance has shifted and they need help. Seeking help should not be a last resort but a proactive step to achieve better balance and health. Listen to your instincts and get help to support your child as soon as you realize this balance has tipped and your child is not responsive to the contract or your parenting toolbox.

Summary:

1. The majority of children, teens, and adults can enjoy digital use and achieve a balance in their life between digital use and non-digital life.

2. Overuse of digital devices can lead to sleep deprivation, anxiety, depression, and obesity.

3. Some children, teens, and adults cannot effectively manage their digital usage and develop signs of addiction, showing withdrawal symptoms when they are not allowed to access digital items. Use the Internet Addiction Test (www.netaddiction.com/internet-addiction-test), to assess if your child's digital use has become addictive.

4. When you feel the balance is tipping toward digital overuse and your child is suffering, seek professional help. Appendix P lists resources for finding a professional that can help.

5. Present the idea of seeking help from a professional as a hopeful proactive step, not a punitive one. The need for professional help should not be seen as a "failure" on the child's part but rather a sign that the team needs support and new skills.

6. Trust your instincts and seek help early before behavioral patterns become extremely ingrained.

Twelve

Conclusion

The May family, who we met in the first chapter, devoted several weeks to designing their digital family plan. Within ten days of implementing it they started reporting concrete benefits. Three months after implementation they came in for a follow-up visit and noted that the digital family plan was one of the best things they had ever done as parents. Dee summarized their feelings: "John and I thought designing a digital family plan would be a huge war and actually alienate us even further from the boys. In fact, we are closer than before. We are all on the same page about the expectations. I no longer need to sneak around to see what the boys are doing in their rooms. They do most of the screen time in the family room, and we interact much more now that we have instituted digital-free family time and the contract. We have found that keeping the cell phones out of the boys' rooms has had the added benefit of them sleeping much better and being better rested. I am no longer fearful of the digital world and am much more hopeful that my daughter can follow in the boys' footsteps. We are a happier family."

The Parker family, who we also met in the first chapter, designed a digital family plan too. It took this family a month to devise the plan, and after some initial changes during the first week of the plan, they reported an overall change in atmosphere in the house after two weeks. Steve describes the process:

"Working on a digital family plan, Mary and I realized how different our feelings were about digital access for Ashley. Some of the stress we had all felt was really coming from Mary and I being in different places about what was okay for Ashley. It took us a while to come to a place where we agreed on what was acceptable for Ashley to do and when, and then we could really develop a digital family plan with Ashley. There is definitely less stress in the house now that Mary and I are on the same page, and we can parent Ashley about digital use without so much stress and second guessing. Ashley seems much more willing to follow the rules and to talk with us about what is going on with her. We are all more relaxed with our digital plan in place."

The digital world is the new parenting frontier. Parents throughout time have encountered new technology (the telephone, record players) and have learned to navigate it and establish parenting techniques to address the new challenges. Although we do not have a parenting model from our parents of how to address these digital parenting issues, we already have many skills we need to confront this new frontier. Parents do not need to recreate an entire parenting strategy to address the challenges presented by the digital world. Parents can utilize many basic techniques they have applied to other daily parenting issues and organize a comprehensive plan to manage the challenges and benefits presented by this new technology. Instead of being overwhelmed or paralyzed with fear by this new technology, parents can embrace it, armed with their parenting toolbox, and establish a sound plan to support their family's digital usage.

Using the ten principles for creating a digital family plan, you can develop a sound, enforceable, and balanced plan for your family. Each principle provides a foundation upon which you can build the restrictions, expectations, consequences, and reinforcers that will help maintain the success of the plan. The guiding principles are:

1. Create a positive digital floor plan
2. Know the technology—the pros and cons
3. Develop digital access restrictions
4. Develop digital access expectations
5. Establish a digital access contract
6. Be consistent within yourself and as a team
7. Give reinforcement and consequences
8. Maintain balance
9. Practice what you preach
10. Know when enough is enough and when to seek help

The plan is not static but can evolve and change as your family's needs change. The plan can begin with a high level of restrictions and monitoring and can change to be less restrictive as your child ages and you feel comfortable giving them more freedom. The ultimate goal is to support your child in becoming a good and safe digital consumer who can create balance between the digital world and other life demands independently.

Knowledge is power. With the information in this book you can move forward and parent without fear. You can embrace the new digital frontier as a great opportunity for your family and a parenting challenge that can be overcome with the skills you already own and some simple principles and planning. Take the time now to develop the foundation for your digital family plan and it will pay dividends in the future. You can parent without fear in this digital era; support your child in becoming a good and safe cybercitizen who seeks balance between the digital world and the real world. Embrace this new parenting frontier!

Digital Floor Plan
Worksheet

Overview: The Digital Floor Plan of your home can support your parenting around digital issues or sabotage it. Taking the time to organize a sensitive and thoughtful digital floor plan is essential. This floor plan will be the foundation upon which your digital parenting plan will be built.

Step 1: Sketch your home floor plan on a piece of paper. Use a separate box for each floor. Only sketch rooms (no halls or bathrooms are needed).

Step 2: Using the sketch you have made and a blue marker, outline all the rooms that are family focused or where the family congregates throughout the day (kitchen, dining room, family room).

Step 3: Using the same sketch you have made, use a red marker to make an "X" in all rooms where there is a television or computer with Internet access, and locations where you charge your cell phones or other digital devices.

Step 4: Look at your sketch. It is optimal if all your red "X's" are located in blue rooms or central family locations. If you have red "X's" in rooms that are not blue, you do not have a digital floor plan that will set your family up for digital success. Consider if you can move the digital devices out of the rooms that are not blue and into the blue or central family locations.

Step 5: Sketch another rendition of your family floor plan trying to have all digital access points, including charging stations, in central family locations.

Step 6: Answer the following questions to ascertain if you have an optimal digital floor plan for your family.

1. Do you have digital devices only in family central locations?   Y N
2. Are the digital devices in locations you can monitor?   Y N
3. Do you have a charging station that is not in a bedroom for computers and cell phones?   Y N
4. Have you organized a way for your family to wake up in the morning that does not involve use of a cell phone?   Y N
5. Are all televisions out of children's bedrooms?   Y N
6. Do computers in children's rooms only have word processing capability and no Internet access?   Y N
7. If computers have Internet access in children's rooms have you developed a monitoring plan?   Y N

Step 7: If you answered yes to all the previous questions, you have designed a sensitive digital floor plan that will support your parenting success around digital issues. If you answered no to any of the above questions, take some time to evaluate if you could make changes. You want to answer yes to all the questions. Remember that a digital floor plan is the foundation of your parenting on digital issues.

Appendix B

Resources for Learning about the Internet, Cyber Safety, and Cyberbullying

Resources for Information on the Internet and Internet Safety:
1. www.staysafeonline.org
2. www.stopthinkconnect.org
3. www.us-cert.gov/Home-Network-Security
4. www.lorigetz.com
5. www.cybersmart.org
6. www.commonsensemedia.org

Published Guides for Parents on the Internet:
1. Edgington, Shawn Marie. 2011. *The Parent's Guide to Texting, Facebook and Social Media.* Dallas, Texas: Brown Books.
2. La Bonet, Jay. 2006. *Parent's Guide to the Internet.* Lulu.com.
3. Levine, John, Baroud, Carol, and Levine Young, Margaret. 2010. *The Internet for Dummies.* Hoboken, New Jersey: IDG Books.
4. Rose, Kathryn. 2010. *The Parent's Guide to Facebook: Tips and strategies to protect your children on the world's largest social network.* CreateSpace.

5. Steyer, James. 2012. *Talking Back to Facebook: The Common Sense Media Guide to Raising Kids in the Digital Age.* New York: Simon and Schuster.

Note: Because of the dynamic nature of the Internet, any web addresses or links contained in this book may have changed since publication and may no longer be valid.

Digital-Focused Magazines

CPU Computer Power User Magazine
iPhone Life Magazine
MacLife Magazine
Mac World Magazine
Maximum PC Magazine
PC Magazine
Smart Computing Magazine
Wired

Daily Schedule Worksheet

Overview: Use this worksheet to evaluate your child's daily schedule and assess how much free time he or she has each day. First enter in the time committed to school, homework, and other activities as indicated to determine potential free time. Next divide the free time among sleep (use Appendix E to assess how much sleep is needed by age), eating (family meals are best), and non-digital time prior to bed (30-45 minutes are recommended) and then determine how much free screen time may be available each day. The schedule will reveal how much scheduled time your child has daily. Remember that the potential free time does not all need to be devoted to digital access. You and your child can negotiate how this time should be used as you complete this worksheet together.

Daily Schedule Worksheet

I. *Complete the Schedule: Fill in the amount of time your child spends daily in each activity listed. If his or her schedule varies significantly each day (soccer practice only 3 days a week for 2 hours), complete a schedule for each day. Copy the worksheet for use multiple times.*

Day _____ (Mon, Tues, Weds, Thurs, Fri, Sat, Sun)

Amount of time per activity per day:
Breakfast:
School hours:
Transportation to and from school:
Getting ready for school:
Afterschool sport:
Afterschool hobby:
Homework:
Family meal:
Family time:
Wind-down time before bed:
Sleep time:
Total of committed time: _____ subtracted from 24 hours = _____ (potential free screen time)

II. *Assess Balance of Activities:*
Fill in the amount of time spent each day in each activity area. A balanced day will have time spent in each activity area every day. It may not be possible to achieve balance each day, but the idea is to have a balanced week. As you complete the schedule for various days, you will want to look for this balance. Ensure that each day has sufficient sleep and pre-sleep wind-down time. Don't forget the importance of time to be bored.

Total school and homework time:
Total afterschool sports/physical activity:
Total family time (including family meals):
Total sleep (check Appendix E to see if this amount is right):
Wind-down time prior to sleep:
Total non-digital free time (time to be bored and explore):

If balance is not achieved in the schedule or there are some activities the child spends not enough time in each day, assess how to establish better balance and variety. If they have a lot of free time, some of this time can be directed to the activity areas that are not being filled. If they have no free time, evaluate if they are overscheduled and/or if they are using their time efficiently.

Appendix E

Sleep Requirements by Age

Age	Total Hours of Sleep (including naps)
Newborns (0-2 months)	12-18 hours
Infants (3-11 months)	14-15 hours
Toddlers (1-3 years)	12-14 hours
Preschoolers (3-5 years)	11-13 hours
School-age children (5-10 years)	10-11 hours
Teens (10-17 years old)	8.5-9.25 hours
Adults	7-9 hours

Source: National Sleep Foundation

Worksheet for Writing Restrictions

Overview: Restrictions for digital usage will address the type of digital item, the amount of time it can be accessed, the type of material that can be accessed, contingencies that need to be met to earn access, the time of day the items can be accessed, and the location they can be accessed in. Remember that digital access is best when:

1. It is monitored in a central family location, such as a kitchen or family room.
2. It occurs at a time of day when parents will be present to monitor usage.
3. A kitchen timer or stopwatch is used as a guide to time.
4. It does not occur in the bedroom at night.
5. You create a non-digital buffer time at least 30 minutes prior to going to bed.

Directions: _Write your restriction on the worksheet and then answer the following questions. If you answer yes to all the questions, your restriction is probably a good one. If you answer no to any of the questions, rework your restriction so you can answer yes to all the questions. Copy the worksheet and complete this activity for each restriction._

*Restriction 1: _____

_____

-Is the restriction phrased positively?   Y N
-Does it have minimal verbiage?   Y N
-Can the restriction be monitored?   Y N
-Does the restriction take into account the five key rules
listed above?   Y N
-Does the restriction relate to the type, amount, location, or
contingencies for digital use?   Y N

*(repeat for each restriction)

Appendix G

Popular Social Media Sites and Apps for Children and Teens

The following list details social media platforms (sites and apps) that are popular with children and teens today. All the platforms listed have issues related to privacy and content. Most of the sites and applications are free, however, some have associated fees. Most platforms list 13 as the minimum age for users, however, little validation of age is performed.

Facebook: Allows users to create a profile page and "friend" others with whom they can share photos and comments.

Twitter: Users can post short (140 characters or less) messages that are sent to their "followers". These messages are called "tweets" and many sports and film celebrities tweet regularly.

Instagram: This platform allows individuals to edit and share photos and 15 second videos with either a select group of people or publicly.

Snapchat: An application where users can send photos to friends that will "disappear" in a certain period of time. However, a screenshot of the photo can be taken before it disappears and there is evidence that Snapchats can be recovered.

Tumblr: Allows users to create a short blog with photos and videos that can be seen by a select group of followers or made public.

Google+: A platform similar to Facebook that allows users to identify friends and circles of friends to communicate with including the option of video chats in "hangouts" with select friends.

Vine: An application that allows users to post six second videos that replay to be seen by followers or publicly.

Wanelo: A site that focuses on fashion, shopping and social networking. Users can see the most popular fashion and shopping trends and can develop their own style and buy items.

Kik Messenger: An application that allows for texting without fees or message limits.

Oovoo: This application provides video, voice, and messaging services for free for groups of up to 12 people.

Pheed: Social application that allows users to post videos and text that they maintain the rights to and can charge others to view. There can be a fee associated with this site.

Ask.fm: Site that allows individuals to post questions and answers on an array of topics that can be publicly viewed.

Chatroulette: A site that allows users to chat with others randomly.

Expectations for Inclusion in Digital Use Contract

Overview: A list of expectations that should be considered in all Digital Use Contracts follows:

1. Treat others online with kindness and respect.
2. Let parents know immediately when someone has treated you unkindly online.
3. Let parents know immediately if a friend is being treated unkindly online.
4. Let parents know immediately if someone online, even if you don't know them, is treating someone unkindly or being treated unkindly.
5. Talk to your parents about anything that makes you feel uncomfortable that happens online or about anything you do not understand.
6. Share only tasteful pictures online that have been approved by parents first.
7. Never assume that a photo or message will be deleted by a friend or "disappear." Anyone can take a photo of a screen shot and keep it or send it to others.

8. Share only general information about yourself online, but never disclose your home address, phone number, or school name to those you do not know.

9. Do not give out personal information such as address, telephone number, parents' work addresses/telephone numbers, or the name and location of your school without parents' permission.

10. Never agree to meet someone you "met" online without first checking with your parents. If your parents agree to the meeting, be sure that it is in a public place, and bring your mother or father along.

11. Do not respond to any messages that are mean or in any way make you feel uncomfortable. It is not your fault if you get a message like that. If you do, tell your parents right away so they can contact the service provider.

12. Do not give out your Internet password(s) to anyone (even your best friends) other than your parents.

13. Check with your parents before downloading or installing software or doing anything that could possibly hurt your computer or jeopardize your family's privacy.

14. Be a good cybercitizen and do not do anything that hurts others or is against the law.

Checklist for Digital
Use Contract

Directions: Use the following checklist to ensure your Digital Use Contract has all the necessary components to make it complete and effective.

I. Restrictions:

Y N Does your contract contain restrictions?

Y N Are the restrictions stated positively?

Y N Do the restrictions have minimal verbiage?

Y N Are the restrictions able to be monitored?

Y N Do the restrictions address time limits for digital usage?

Y N Do the restrictions address location of digital access? (central location is best)

Y N Do the restrictions allow for a digital-free time prior to bed?

Y N Do the restrictions address not having digital items in the bedroom at night?

II. Expectations:

Y N Does the contract contain digital expectations for cyber behavior?

Y N Are the expectations stated positively?

Y N Is minimal verbiage used?
Y N Are the following recommended expectations included?

1. Use only respectful language (no curse words).
2. Treat others online with kindness and respect.
3. Let parents know immediately when someone has treated you unkindly online.
4. Let parents know immediately if a friend is being treated unkindly online.
5. Let parents know immediately if someone online, even if you don't know them, is treating someone unkindly or being treated unkindly.
6. Tell your parents about anything that makes you feel uncomfortable that happens online or about anything you do not understand.
7. Share only tasteful pictures online that have been approved by parents first.
8. Share only general information about yourself online, but never disclose your home address, phone number, or school name to those you do not know.

III. Monitoring:

Y N Does the contract describe the type of monitoring techniques that will occur?
Y N Are these stated clearly and in positive language?
Y N Are any of the following monitoring techniques included? (they don't all have to be, but if you will be using any of these you should indicate this on the contract)

1. We will periodically check what information is available about you online.
2. We will periodically check the history of sites you have visited on the computer and on your mobile phone.
3. We will periodically check your social network site profile.

4. We will friend you on any social media sites you join.
5. We will periodically look at the texts you send.
6. We expect to be notified about any passwords needed to access your computer or mobile accounts.

IV. Consequences:

Y N Does the contract contain consequences?

Y N Are they stated in positive language?

Y N Can the restrictions be enforced?

Y N Are they not overly punitive?

Y N Are they not overly permissive?

V. Length of Contract:

Y N Does the contract specify for what length of time it will be in effect?

Y N Is there an indication that the contract will be revisited when any member of the team has a concern?

VI. Contract Format:

Y N Is the contract presented in a formalized manner that looks official?

Y N Is the contract visually clear?

Y N Is there room for the child and all team members to sign the contract?

Y N Can you make copies of the contract to present to members to review and troubleshoot around?

Y N Will you be able to produce copies of the contract once signed so at least one copy can be posted near a digital access point as a reminder and another can be stored for safekeeping?

Contract with Child's
Notes and Questions

Overview: Below is a sample contract. The parents gave the contract to their daughter, Jane, to review prior to formalizing it. Her questions and thoughts are indicated in bold. It is instructive to look at what questions a child raises. It is also empowering to allow your child to review and make comments about the contract prior to it being formalized. A formalized contract that incorporates Jane's comments follows in Appendix L.

Digital Use Contract for the Dillon Family

The digital world has many benefits and some risks. We have developed this plan to support you in reaping the benefits of the digital world and to ensure you are a safe and good cybercitizen.

I. **Restrictions:**
1. Jane will be allowed to have 40 minutes of free digital time (Internet, cell phone, iPod, television) after homework is completed in the family room between 4:00 and 7:00 p.m. each night.

2. Jane will set a timer in the kitchen for 40 minutes when she starts her digital time.
3. Jane will always charge her cell phone in the charging station in the kitchen when she gets home after school and will turn the ringer off.
4. Jane will only text or respond to calls before 8:30 at night.
5. Jane will not bring her digital devices into her bedroom at night.
6. Jane will have non-digital wind-down time for at least half an hour before bed.

What if I don't have homework? Do I still get digital free time? Can I use my iPhone as an alarm clock?

II. Expectations:
1. Jane will use only respectful language (no curse words).
2. Jane will treat others online with kindness and respect.
3. Jane will let parents know immediately when someone has treated her unkindly online.
4. Jane will let parents know immediately if a friend is being treated unkindly online.
5. Jane will let parents know immediately if someone online, even if she doesn't know them, is treating someone unkindly or being treated unkindly.
6. Jane will talk to her parents about anything that makes her feel uncomfortable that happens online or about anything she does not understand.
7. Jane will only share tasteful pictures online that have been approved by her parents first.
8. Jane will only share general information about herself online but will never disclose her home address, phone number, or school name to those she does not know.

III. **Monitoring:**

To ensure your safekeeping in the digital world, we will do the following:

1. Use parental controls on the computer and Jane's mobile phone that block, filter, and/or monitor her usage.
2. Use filter systems that set PC game blocking by rating.
3. Use filter systems that limit access by time of day and daily time limits.
4. Use filter systems that provide keystroke and screen captures.
5. Use filter systems that provide detailed and graphical reports of online activity.

Will you tell me what you find from the monitoring? Will you do less monitoring if I am following all the rules?

IV. **Consequences:**

We know you will work hard to follow all the restrictions and meet the expectations in this contract. Below are the consequences we have designed because we realize it is fair for you to know what they are.

1. If Jane engages in digital free time (accessing Facebook or sports websites) before her homework is complete, she will lose her digital free time the next day.
2. If Jane says unkind things or uses curse words online she will not be allowed to go on a social media site for a month.
3. If Jane uses her digital items after bedtime she will lose her digital free time privileges for a week.

V. **Length of Contract:**

1.   This contract will remain in effect until summer break.
2.   If Jane or her parents want to renegotiate the contract, this can be done at any time.
3.   If some part of the contract does not seem to be working, we will meet and discuss how to make it work better.

Signatures on date _____:

_____

Jane

_____

Mom

_____

Dad

_____

Babysitter Molly

Appendix K

List of High-Tech Filtering/Monitoring Software

The filtering/monitoring software listed below is consistently rated as most effective. Visit the website of each product for additional information.

Net NannyWeb Watcher
McAfee Safe Eyes
Profil Parental Filter 2
PC Pandora
Family Protector
Spytech SpyAgent
eBlaster
Spector Pro
Norton Family (no cost)

Source: Tech Media Network (2014)

Official Contract

Overview: A revised Digital Use Contract for the Dillon family follows. The additions and clarifications made after Jane's questions were noted on the draft contract are noted in italics.

Dillon Family Digital Use Contract

I. Restrictions:

1. Jane will be allowed to have 40 minutes of free digital time (Internet, cell phone, iPod, television) after homework is completed in the family room between 4:00 and 7:00 p.m. each night.
2. Jane will set a timer for 40 minutes in the kitchen when she starts her digital time.
3. Jane will always charge her cell phone in the charging station in the kitchen when she gets home after school and will turn the ringer off.
4. Jane will only text or respond to calls during her 40 minutes of free digital access time.
5. Jane will never bring her digital devices into her bedroom at night.

6. Jane will never engage in any digital access at least half an hour before bed.
7. *If Jane doesn't have homework she will still be allowed her digital free access time at the usual time and in the usual location.*
8. *We will supply Jane with a new alarm clock she can select.*
9. *Jane will not use her iPhone as an alarm clock.*

II. Expectations:
1. Jane will use only respectful language (no curse words).
2. Jane will treat others online with kindness and respect.
3. Jane will let parents know immediately when someone has treated her unkindly online.
4. Jane will let parents know immediately if a friend is being treated unkindly online.
5. Jane will let parents know immediately if someone online, even if she doesn't know them, is treating someone unkindly or being treated unkindly.
6. Jane will talk to her parents about anything that makes her feel uncomfortable that happens online or about anything she does not understand.
7. Jane will only share tasteful pictures online that have been approved by her parents first.
8. Jane will only share general information about herself online but will never disclose her home address, phone number or school name to those she does not know.

III. Monitoring:
To ensure your safekeeping in the digital world, we will do the following:

1. Use parental controls on the computer and Jane's mobile phone that block, filter, and/or monitor her usage.

2. Use filter systems that set PC game blocking by rating.
3. Use filter systems that limit access by time of day and daily time limits.
4. Use filter systems that provide keystroke and screen captures.
5. Use filter systems that provide detailed and graphical reports of online activity.
6. *We will update Jane from time to time about what the monitoring shows.*
7. *We will make sure to let Jane know that she is doing a good job when we review the filters, if this is the case.*

IV. Consequences:

We know you will work hard to follow all the restrictions and meet the expectations in this contract. Below are the consequences we have designed because we realize it is fair for you to know what they are.

1. If Jane engages in digital free time (accessing Facebook or sports websites) before her homework is complete, she will lose her digital free time the next day.
2. If Jane says unkind things or uses curse words online she will not be allowed to go on a social media site for a month.
3. If Jane uses digital items after bedtime she will lose her digital free time privileges for one month.

V. Length of Contract:

1. This contract will remain in effect until summer break.
2. If Jane or her parents want to renegotiate the contract, this can be done at any time.
3. If some part of the contract does not seem to be working, we will meet and discuss how to make it work better.

Signatures on date _____:

_____   _____
Jane   Mom

_____   _____
Dad   Babysitter Molly

Daily Schedule Balance Worksheet

Directions: Use this worksheet to assess how balanced your day was. Optimally, a day that has hours spent in all the categories listed below is recommended. In addition, this worksheet allows you to monitor your sleep, which is crucial to feeling balanced. You are also asked to rate your mood. Mood is important to monitor. Feeling down a lot of days can be linked to not getting enough sleep, feeling unbalanced in your day, or other factors as well. The worksheet also asks you to predict if the next day will be balanced. If you find yourself predicting an unbalanced day, you can be proactive and change the day to be more balanced or accept that it will be unbalanced and try to achieve better balance on a subsequent day.

Date _____

Hours spent in school:
Hours spent doing homework:
Hours spent in afterschool sports:
Hours spent with family:
Hours spent doing nothing:

Hours spent on digital free access time:
Hours spent in other activity:
Hours of sleep last night:
Rate your mood (scale of 1 to 5 with 1 being very down, 3 being a normal mood for you, and 5 being very happy):

1. Did today feel balanced (did you get some time in each of the activities listed above and adequate sleep for your age, see Appendix E)?

2. If you answered yes to the above question, good job! What will you do tomorrow to maintain the balance?

3. If you answered no to the above question, what will you do to make tomorrow a better-balanced day?

4. Look at your mood rating for today. If it was a 1 or 2, why do you think this was? What can you do to achieve a higher rating tomorrow? If your rating was a 3-5, why was this and what can you do to maintain this rating tomorrow?

5. Looking ahead to tomorrow, would you guess that it will be a balanced day or not? Why?

Appendix N

Relaxing Activity Sheet

Directions: This information is meant to provide suggestions of activities that can be relaxing and independent as a prequel to sleep. Instead of dozing off with a television turned on or a cell phone in hand, try some of these activities. You may find you fall asleep more quickly and sleep better throughout the night. These activities can also be used during the day at times of stress.

I. Relaxing Image Activity:

Think about a scene that makes you feel safe, happy and relaxed. The image should be one that makes you feel content, but not overly excited. In your mind, review the scene, noting how it looks, with a focus on details and colors. Also think about the sounds, smells and physiological experiences that are present (i.e., breeze that touches your arms, cold, crisp air that enters your nose and mouth). Consider also how the scene makes you feel emotionally and how it affects your muscle tensions. For example, does your heart rate slow when you think about the image? Does your jaw feel less clenched? Is your posture more open and free?

Develop a written script for the scene, focusing on the factors noted above. Write a paragraph about the scene in such a way that would make the experience clear to an outsider. Consider sketching a picture or using a photo of the image to go along with the description.

Practice reading the image description twice a day and consider posting the image in a place where you can view it readily. With practice, the script will become routine and you can conjure it up quickly to help yourself relax or refocus.

II. Breathing Activities:

The goal of breathing activities is to make you more aware of how you breathe and give you some control over your breathing. Focusing on your breathing can be relaxing and can distract you from stressors.

A. Deep Breathing:

1. Lie down or sit in a comfortable chair with good posture. Relax your body as much as possible. Close your eyes and scan your body for tension.
2. Focus on your breathing. Put one hand on the part of your chest or abdomen that rises and falls the most with each breath. If this spot is in your chest you are not utilizing the lower part of your lungs.
3. Put both hands on your abdomen and focus your breathing. Pay attention to how your abdomen rises and falls.
4. Breathe through your nose.
5. Notice if your chest is moving in harmony with your abdomen.
6. Now place one hand on your abdomen and one on your chest.
7. Inhale deeply and slowly through your nose into your abdomen. You should feel your abdomen rise with this inhalation, but your chest should move only a little.
8. Exhale through your mouth counting to 7. Try to keep your mouth, tongue, and jaw relaxed.
9. Relax. Focus on the feeling and sound of long, slow, deep breaths.
10. Repeat the procedure.

Practice the Deep Breathing activity two times a day, or when needed, for 3 to 5 minutes at a time. This activity can be used as a tool when trying to fall asleep.

B. Natural Breathing:

1. Sit or stand using good posture.
2. Breathe through your nose.
3. Inhale. Fill the lower part of your lungs then the middle part, then the upper part.
4. Hold your breath for a few seconds.
5. Exhale slowly.
6. Relax your abdomen and chest.

Practice this activity twice a day for 3-5 minutes. This activity will help you relax and can assist you in falling asleep.

III. Progressive Muscle Relaxation Activity:

This activity is aimed at decreasing the muscle tension you may feel in parts of your body. The activity can be used during self-soothing time or when trying to fall asleep. In this technique, focus on slowly tensing and then relaxing each muscle group in your body. This helps you focus on the difference between muscle tension and relaxation. You can become more aware of physical sensations.

Start by tensing and relaxing the muscles in your toes and pro-gressively working your way up to your neck and head. You can also start with your head and neck and work down to your toes. Tense your muscles for at least five seconds and then relax for 10 to 30 seconds, and repeat. Practice this activity one to two times a day.

Non-Digital Family Games by Age

Preschool (ages 0-5):
Candy Land
Chutes and Ladders
Card games (Go Fish, Old Maid)
Connect Four
Hungry, Hungry Hippo
Memory
Telephone
Twister

Elementary School (ages 6-10):
Apples to Apples Junior
Battleship
Card games (Go Fish, Old Maid, Uno)
Checkers
Chess
Clue Junior
Mad Libs
Parcheesi

Pictionary Junior
Operation
Telephone

Junior High School (ages 11-13):
Pictionary
Apples to Apples
Charades
Life
Monopoly
Card games (Concentration, Hearts, Gin Rummy, Crazy Eights)
Battleship
Chess
Checkers
Chinese Checkers
Telephone
Mad Libs
Jenga
Puzzles

High School (ages 14-17):
Battleship
Card games (Rummy, Rummy 500, Kings in the Corner, Ninety-Nine)
Charades
Chess
Life
Monopoly
Pictionary
Puzzles

How to Find a
Professional to Help

Questions to Ask a Professional

I. How to find a professional to help:
American Psychiatric Association (www.psych.org):
This is an organization of psychiatrists who hold an MD degree. Information about psychiatrists can be obtained on this site.

American Psychological Association (www.apa.org):
This is an organization of psychologists who hold a doctorate (PhD, PsyD, EdD) in the field of psychology or a related field. To find more about psychologists visit this website. The site also has a Psychology Help Center that allows you to enter your location to see a list of APA-member psychologists in your area and their profiles.

American Association of Marriage and Family Therapists (www.aamft.org):
This is an organization of marriage and family therapists that have a master's degree in the field. The site contains a

Therapist Locator that helps you find a marriage and family therapist in your area.

Association of Licensed Clinical Social Workers (www. socialworkers.org):
This is an association of social workers. The site contains information about social workers and links to find a social worker in your local area.

II. Questions to ask a professional:
1. Have you worked with families that are having trouble managing digital access and creating balance?
2. What is your clinical orientation?
3. What kind of insurance do you accept?
4. What is your hourly fee?
5. What is your background and training?
6. Where is your office? What are your office hours?
6. Will you be meeting with the parents and the child?
7. How many sessions will you take to assess the situation?
8. How many sessions do you think treatment will take?
9. How long will it be before you can see us?
10. Will you see the whole family together for the first session?
11. Is there any information you would like us to gather and bring to the first session?
12. Is there anything we should be doing in anticipation of our first meeting?
13. Are there any other questions we should ask?

References

Bourne, E. J. 1995. *The Anxiety and Phobia Workbook.* Oakland: New Harbinger Publications.

Common Sense Media. "Digital literacy and citizenship in the 21st century: A common sense media interpretation." March 2011.

Common Sense Media. "Protecting our kids' privacy in a digital world." A common sense public policy brief. December 2011.

Common Sense Media. "The impact of media on child and adolescent health: Executive summary and systematic review." December 2008.

Common Sense Media. "Zero to eight: children's media use in America." October 2011.

Common Sense Media. "Zero to eight: children's media use in America." October 2013.

Common Sense Media. "11 sites and apps kids are heading to after Facebook." September 2013.

Cyberbullying Research Center. "Cyberbullying: Neither an epidemic nor a rarity." March 21, 2013.

David, L., and Uhrenholdt, K. 2010. *The Family Dinner: Great Ways to Connect with Your Kids, One Meal at a Time.* New York: Grand Central Life and Style.

Family Online Safety Institute. "Who needs parental controls? A survey of answers and attitudes and use of parental controls." September 14, 2011.

Ferber, R. 1985. *Solve Your Child's Sleep Problems.* New York: Simon & Schuster.

International Center for Media and the Public Agenda. "24 Hours: Unplugged." April 11, 2010.

Janis, I. L. 1972. *Victims of Groupthink: A Psychological Study of Foreign-Policy Decisions and Fiascoes.* Oxford: Houghton Mifflin.

Janis, I. L. 1982. *Groupthink: Psychological Studies of Policy Decisions and Fiascoes.* Boston: Wadsworth.

Kaiser Family Foundation. "Generation M2: Media in the Lives of 8- to18-Year Olds." January 20, 2010.

Lenhart, A., Madden, M., Smith, A., Purcell, K., Zickuhr, K., and Rainie, L. "Teens, kindness and cruelty on social media sites." Pew Research Institute. November 9, 2011.

Mindell, J.A. 1997. *Get Your Child to Sleep through the Night.* New York: HarperCollins.

Mindell, J. A., and Owens, J.A. 2010. *A Clinical Guide to Pediatric Sleep: Diagnosis and Management of Sleep Problems,* 2nd ed. Philadelphia: Wolters Kluwer/Lippincott Williams & Wilkins.

Mitchell, K.J., Finkelhor, D., and Wolak, J. 2007. "Youth internet users at risk for most serious online sexual solicitations." *American Journal of Preventative Medicine,* 32 (6): 532-7.

Mogel, W. 2001. *The Blessings of a Skinned Knee.* New York: Penguin Group.

O'Keeffe, G.S., and Clarke-Pearson, K. 2011. "The impact of social media on children, adolescents and families." *Pediatrics,* 127 (4): 800-4.

Pew Internet and American Life Project. "Teens' parents and their technology profile." November 9, 2011.

Polos, P.J., Bhat, S., Smith, I., Kabak, B., Neiman, I., Sillari, J., Chokroverty, S., and Seyffert, M. "The Effect of Sleep Time Related Information and Communication Technology (STRICT) on Sleep Patterns and Daytime Functioning in Children and Young Adults: A Pilot Study." Presented at CHEST 2010, the 76th annual meeting of the American

College of Chest Physicians (ACCP), Vancouver, Canada, November 1, 2010.

Smith, A. "Americans and text messaging." Pew Internet and Family Life. September 19, 2011.

Smith, A. "Why Americans use social media." Pew Internet and Family Life. November 15, 2011.

Willard, N. 2007. *Cyber-Safe Kids, Cyber-Savvy Teens: Helping Young People Learn to Use the Internet Safely and Responsibly.* Hoboken: Jossey-Bass.

Willard, N. 2006. *Cyberbullying and Cyberthreats: Responding to the Challenge of Online Social Cruelty, Threats and Distress.* Eugene: Center for Safe and Responsible Internet Use.

Zimmerman, F.J. "Children's media use and sleep problems: Issues and unanswered questions." Kaiser Family Foundation. Research Brief, June 2008.

About the Author

Dr. Winifred Lender is a licensed psychologist in private practice. She works with individuals and families around issues related to managing the real world and virtual world, anxiety and depression. She has seen a significant rise in concern related to developing plans to manage the digital lives of children and teens over the past decade and presents on this topic to parent and teacher groups.

Dr. Lender received her bachelor of science degree form Cornell University and her MSEd and PhD degrees from the University of Pennsylvania. She completed a fellowship at the Children's Hospital/University of Pennsylvania School of Medicine in Pediatric Psychology. She is a past president of the Santa Barbara County Psychological Association.

More information about Dr. Lender is available on her website, www.drwinifredlender.com.